Abrams
She

J.J. Abrams

by Barbara Sheen

LUCENT BOOKS

A part of Gale, Cengage Learning

GALE
CENGAGE Learning·

Farmington Hills, Mich • San Francisco • New York • Waterville, Maine
Meriden, Conn • Mason, Ohio • Chicago

© 2015 Gale, Cengage Learning

WCN:01-100-101

LIBRARY OF CONGRESS CATALOGING-IN-PUBLICATION DATA

Sheen, Barbara.
   J. J. Abrams / by Barbara Sheen.
     pages cm. -- (People in the news)
   Includes bibliographical references and index.
   ISBN 978-1-4205-1249-6 (hardcover)
   1. Abrams, J. J. (Jeffrey Jacob), 1966---Juvenile literature. 2. Television producers and directors--United States--Biography--Juvenile literature. 3. Motion picture producers and directors--United States--Biography--Juvenile literature. I. Title.
   PN1998.3.A27S54 2015
   791.4302'33092--dc23
   [B]
                                    2014033028

Lucent Books
27500 Drake Rd.
Farmington Hills, MI 48331

ISBN-13: 978-1-4205-1249-6
ISBN-10: 1-4205-1249-8

Printed in the United States of America
1 2 3 4 5 6 7 19 18 17 16 15

Contents

ame and celebrity are alluring. People are drawn to those who walk in fame's spotlight, whether they are known for great accomplishments or for notorious deeds. The lives of the famous pique public interest and attract attention, perhaps because their experiences seem in some ways so different from, yet in other ways so similar to, our own.

Newspapers, magazines, and television regularly capitalize on this fascination with celebrity by running profiles of famous people. For example, television programs such as *Entertainment Tonight* devote all their programming to stories about entertainment and entertainers. Magazines such as *People* fill their pages with stories of the private lives of famous people. Even newspapers, newsmagazines, and television news frequently delve into the lives of well-known personalities. Despite the number of articles and programs, few provide more than a superficial glimpse at their subjects.

Lucent's People in the News series offers young readers a deeper look into the lives of today's newsmakers, the influences that have shaped them, and the impact they have had in their fields of endeavor and on other people's lives. The subjects of the series hail from many disciplines and walks of life. They include authors, musicians, athletes, political leaders, entertainers, entrepreneurs, and others who have made a mark on modern life and who, in many cases, will continue to do so for years to come.

These biographies are more than factual chronicles. Each book emphasizes the contributions, accomplishments, or deeds that have brought fame or notoriety to the individual and shows how that person has influenced modern life. Authors portray their subjects in a realistic, unsentimental light. For example, Bill Gates—cofounder of the software giant Microsoft—has been instrumental in making personal computers the most vital tool of the modern age. Few dispute his business savvy, his perseverance, or his technical expertise, yet critics say he is ruthless in his dealings with competitors and driven more by his desire to maintain Microsoft's dominance in the computer industry than by an interest in furthering technology.

In these books, young readers will encounter inspiring stories about real people who achieved success despite enormous obstacles. Oprah Winfrey—one of the most powerful, most watched, and wealthiest women in television history—spent the first six years of her life in the care of her grandparents while her unwed mother sought work and a better life elsewhere. Her adolescence was colored by pregnancy at age fourteen, rape, and sexual abuse.

Each author documents and supports his or her work with an array of primary and secondary source quotations taken from diaries, letters, speeches, and interviews. All quotes are footnoted to show readers exactly how and where biographers derive their information and provide guidance for further research. The quotations enliven the text by giving readers eyewitness views of the life and accomplishments of each person covered in the People in the News series.

In addition, each book in the series includes photographs, annotated bibliographies, timelines, and comprehensive indexes. For both the casual reader and the student researcher, the People in the News series offers insight into the lives of today's newsmakers—people who shape the way we live, work, and play in the modern age.

The Multi-Hyphenate

J. Abrams began making movies when he was a little boy, and he has never stopped. This curly-haired, bespectacled Hollywood powerhouse is known as a "multi-hyphenate" because of his many talents and occupations. Abrams juggles being a television and movie writer–director–producer–composer with ease. As Steven McPherson, former president of ABC Entertainment, explains: "A lot of people in Hollywood have one great idea, one great movie in them. J.J. gives you four ideas over lunch. Plus, he's talking about the soundtrack, the amusement park ride, the video game. He thinks about the whole world of entertainment."[1]

Abrams not only wears multiple hats but also seems to thrive on multitasking, which may be one reason he is among the busiest and most successful people in Hollywood. Damon Lindelof, who cocreated the television series *Lost* with Abrams, says: "He has to have six or seven things going on to activate him. It energizes him creatively."[2]

Abrams is best known for being the mastermind behind television mystery series such as *Lost* and *Fringe*, and popular science-fiction films such as *Star Trek Into Darkness*. But Abrams's projects cannot be easily classified. He loves all types of movies and television programs, and it shows in his work, which includes action-adventure films such as *Armageddon* and *Mission: Impossible—Ghost Protocol*, as well as heartfelt dramas such as the film *Regarding Henry* and the television series *Felicity*.

A naturally funny man, he also created comedies such as the film *Taking Care of Business* and the television series *What About Brian?* Spy dramas such as the television series *Alias* and *Undercovers*, and crime dramas such as *Person of Interest*, are also part of his résumé, as are eerie horror movies such as *Cloverfield* and

J.J. Abrams poses with a fan dressed as the logo of his production company, Bad Robot, at a 2003 event in London, England.

Super 8. And, these are just a partial list of his creations. There are also the science-fiction television series *Almost Human, Revolution*, and *Believe*, and the latest film in the *Star Wars* series, *Star Wars: Episode VII*.

Some of Abrams's creations have been great successes, while others have not done as well. But on the whole, Abrams has made more hits than misses. Says blogger and communications expert Brendan Reilly: "He [Abrams] has consistently delivered high-quality products that have pleased audiences and reviewers alike. J.J. Abrams has built a strong brand on the back of hard work, talent and creativity."[3]

Common Elements

Despite the variety of his work, all of Abrams's handiworks share common elements that help make them hits. Typically they are emotional stories filled with intrigue and surprising plot twists. "I've always liked working on stories that . . . are relatable [mixed] with something insane," he explains. "The most exciting thing for me is crossing that bridge between something we know is real and something that is extraordinary. The thing for me has always been how you cross that bridge."[4]

Abrams's characters, too, share common elements. Just like real people, his characters are multilayered, complex. He insists that even the most action-packed stories will not succeed without characters that viewers care about. As he explains: "It's all about connecting to the heart and soul of your characters. Once you do that, it doesn't matter what the genre is. . . . All that matters is that you've found a way to emotionally engage the audience."[5]

A Modest Man

His many awards are proof that Abrams understands his audiences. As of 2014, he has been nominated for twenty-four different awards and won thirteen. The wins include one Emmy award; four American Society of Composers, Authors, and Publishers awards; one Academy of Science Fiction, Fantasy and Horror Films award; one Hollywood Film Festival award; two Producers Guild of America awards, one of which was the lifetime achievement award in television; one Spike SCREAM award; one British SFX award; and one Writers Guild award. In addition, he has been named to *Forbes* magazine's list of the one hundred most influential people in Hollywood.

Despite his many accolades, Abrams has not let his success go to his head. In fact, he is modest about his achievements and quick to give credit to his cast and crew. As he told an interviewer:

The amazing thing is you work for years trying to write stuff that works, and then all of a sudden you get paid to do that, and what I realized was that nothing changes. I'm exactly the same goofball, I'm still sitting in the same room, I've got the same computer, the same thoughts in my head. I always thought when I was a kid that if I got my name on the screen I could die happy. And I think there's a certain level of truth to that. But there isn't a day when I don't feel disbelief that I get to do this.[6]

Although he is modest about his achievements, there is no doubt that Abrams has worked hard to get to where he is. Becoming a filmmaker was his lifelong dream, and he has spent most of his life thus far pursuing that dream. Abrams started making movies when he was eight years old. It was his passion then, and it still is. He loves what he does, and it shows in his work. In fact, he still gets the same feeling of wonder from filmmaking that he did as a child, and he feels incredibly lucky to do what he does. The best part of his job, he says, is:

Being able to take the ideas that occur to me and not let them vanish. To go to the set of something that was in my head. It's a total narcissistic [egocentric] joy to have some private little pleasure, through a lucky stream of events, become tangible, so that you can actually walk on it and touch it. It's cool to bring something to life, whether it's a song or a video. But to do it and have it embraced by millions of people all over the world . . . that's insane.[7]

Chapter 1

Unlimited Possibilities

Jeffrey Jacob Abrams was born on June 27, 1966, in New York City. His parents, Gerald and Carol Abrams, gave him the nickname "J.J." at birth, and that is the name he goes by to this day. He was the older of two children. His sister, Tracy, came into the world four years after J.J. At the time of J.J.'s birth, his father was an account executive for the CBS television network and his mother was a housewife.

The family relocated to Pacific Palisades, California, in 1971. There, Gerald and Carol both became successful television producers. Little J.J. was a bright, chubby boy with a vivid imagination. He describes his younger self as "not a very successful kid,"[8] largely because he was a bit of an oddball and a poor athlete.

A Precocious Child

More advanced than other children his age, J.J. remembers learning to read "at a very early age. Like, creepy young. I remember being in the crib, reading. My parents were very impressed."[9]

As he matured, he preferred making up stories and acting them out to sports and childish games. His lack of interest in ordinary juvenile activities did not concern his family. They thought he was special and tried to nurture his creativity even when J.J.'s behavior disturbed one of his elementary school teachers. Tracy recalls one incident:

J.J. Abrams was raised in Southern California, the world's movie capital. His parents moved the family to Pacific Palisades, California, in 1971 and became successful television producers.

[The teacher called and said,] "Dodgeball is a very important sport here in Los Angeles and, during recess, that's what the kids do. But that's not what J.J. does. . . . He ties a red cape around his neck and goes flying around the schoolyard making up stories."

My mother sort of said, "Okay. Is there anything else?" . . . And the teacher said, "No," and my mother said, "Thank you." And, of course, the conversation never went beyond that; she was not about to stop her little boy from running around making up stories.[10]

Who Is Greg Grunberg?

J. J. Abrams and Greg Grunberg have been best friends for more than forty years. Grunberg was born July 11, 1966, in Los Angeles. As a child, he often starred in J.J.'s home movies. Doing so made him want to become an actor.

Early in his career Grunberg worked in television commercials. To supplement his income, he started a successful frozen-yogurt delivery business. More recently, he cocreated a phone app that sends discount coupons to smart phones. He also founded and plays drums in the rock band Band From TV, composed of television actors.

As an actor, Grunberg has appeared in more than twenty films and in numerous television shows. Just as in childhood, Abrams often casts Grunberg in his projects. Grunberg had roles in the Abrams projects *Felicity*, *Alias*, *Lost*, and *Mission: Impossible III*. However, Grunberg is best known for the role of Matt Parkman in the television series *Heroes*.

Grunberg is married to Elizabeth Wershow. They have three sons, one of whom has epilepsy. Because of his son's disorder, Grunberg is very active in raising public awareness about epilepsy and in raising money for epilepsy research.

Greg Grunberg and J.J. Abrams attend a Los Angeles Lakers game in 2009. The two men have been best friends for more than forty years.

His uniqueness made J.J. stand out from many of his peers, and not everyone accepted him. Despite this, J.J. found a kindred spirit among his kindergarten classmates—a boy named Greg Grunberg, who has been his best friend ever since. Grunberg, an actor, often appears in Abrams's productions. Like J.J.'s parents, Grunberg thought his friend was exceptional: "It was obvious immediately that J.J. was brilliant. . . . I remember, when we were about five or seven, my dad took us out for pizza and pulled out a napkin and said, 'J.J., I want to sign you, I want to be your manager!'"[11]

A Special Relationship

Abrams's parents and Grunberg were not the only ones J.J. impressed. His maternal grandfather, Henry Kelvin, doted on him. "Carol's father [Kelvin] never had any sons," Gerald Abrams explains. "And he took a special interest in J.J. . . . They had a very, very close relationship."[12]

Kelvin owned an electronics business. He also had a workshop where he and J.J. took apart and put together small electronic devices to see how they worked. This sparked J.J.'s lifelong interest in science and technology. As he recalls,

My grandfather was a huge inspiration. He was the owner of an electronics company, and after World War II he sold surplus radio and electronics kits to schools.

We would spend hours building and soldering [repairing] things. As a young kid, it's so inspirational to see that you can build things . . . that you can attach the motor to a wire and make something work. My interest in technology and science actually came from his explanations of how radios and transistors work.[13]

Kelvin also introduced J.J. to old-fashioned paper crafts, such as printing with a letterpress, silk-screening, bookbinding, and box making, all of which Abrams still practices today. In fact, he owns a manual letterpress machine that he uses to make greeting cards.

I'm obsessed with printing. I'm obsessed with silk-screening and bookbinding and box making. When I was a kid, I was always, like, taking apart boxes and stuff.

And last night . . . I took apart the Kleenex box. I was just looking at it. And I'm telling you . . . It's a beautiful thing . . . when you look at the box, and you sort of see how it works.[14]

Little Magician

Another interest that J.J. and his grandfather shared was magic. Kelvin took J.J. to a magic store, where he bought the boy simple tricks. When J.J. mastered the tricks, he performed them for his family. He adored putting on shows, but even more, he loved making his audience believe something unreal was real. "There was something about magic, about seeing that little disbelief in their eyes," he explains. "I loved creating any kind of illusions."[15]

J.J. became an accomplished magician. By the time he was ten years old, he was putting on impromptu magic shows at school and performing at birthday parties for young children. Even now, as an adult, he frequently does coin tricks, card tricks, and other sleight-of-hand for the cast and crew working on his films and television projects. As a matter of fact, the bathroom door in his office at Bad Robot (the production company he created) is hidden behind a bookcase that can be accessed only by pressing on a large book about magic.

During one trip to the magic store, Kelvin bought J.J. a mystery magic box. The sales pitch for the box was that for a cost of fifteen dollars, purchasers got magic tricks worth fifty dollars. The box, which is adorned with a giant question mark, is one of J.J.'s most prized possessions. He never opened it. He says that not knowing what the box contains makes it all the more mysterious and magical because the possibilities of what it holds are limited only by a person's imagination.

Abrams devoted a 2013 TED (Technology, Education, Design) speech to the box—why it was important to him, and why he never opened it:

Gerald and Carol Abrams

J. J. Abrams's parents are also celebrities. Gerald Abrams is a producer who has been nominated for an Emmy award and who has produced more than eighty made-for-television movies, specials, miniseries, and documentaries. He also produced one film, *Hearts of Fire*. He started his own production company, Cypress Point Productions, in 1978. He has worked with many famous actors, including Leonard Nimoy, Ben Vereen, and Christopher Plummer, among others. J.J. cast his father in cameo roles in *Felicity*, *Star Trek*, and *Star Trek Into Darkness*. As of 2014, Gerald Abrams is still working.

J.J.'s mother, Carol Abrams, was also a producer. She produced the Peabody Award–winning television movie *The Ernest Green Story*, based on a true story about the integration of Central High School in Little Rock, Arkansas. She also produced two other made-for-television movies and authored two children's books. She did not become a producer until J.J. was grown. During his childhood, she attended law school at Whittier Law School, graduating as the class valedictorian. She worked as a professor at Whittier before becoming a producer. Carol Abrams died of cancer in 2012 at age sixty-nine.

It represents my grandfather. . . . It represents infinite possibility. It represents hope. It represents potential. And what I love about this box, and what I realize I sort of do in whatever it is that I do, is I find myself drawn to infinite possibility, that sense of potential. And I realize that mystery is the catalyst [stimulus] for imagination. . . .

And I realized, oh my God, mystery boxes are everywhere in what I do! . . .

I realize that that blank page is a magic box, you know? It needs to be filled with something fantastic.

Then there's the thing of mystery in terms of imagination. . . .

And then. . . .

What's a bigger mystery box than a movie theater? . . . You go to the theater, you're just so excited to see anything. The moment the lights go down is often the best part. . . .

[So] the mystery box, in honor of my grandfather, stays closed.[16]

An Inspiring Trip

In addition to visiting magic stores, J.J. and his grandfather often took field trips. When J.J. was eight years old, the two went on a tour of Universal Studios. That trip was especially significant. At the time, Universal Studios was a working studio. Visitors

toured the stars' dressing rooms, saw actual props (small objects that actors use in a play or film), and attended demonstrations on how animation, makeup, and special effects are done. J.J. was captivated by all that he saw. He loved movies, but before this trip he had never thought about how they were made. The idea that individuals make movies, creating giant illusions on film, inspired him. Filmmakers, he realized, are magicians. They make audiences believe all sorts of things. For example, movies make it seem like superheroes can fly, like giant monsters are destroying cities, and like aliens from another planet are about to land on Earth—all illusions.

J.J. wanted to create magic on film, too. He recalls: "When I was a little kid—and even still—I loved magic tricks. When

I saw how movies got made—at least had a glimpse when I went on the Universal Studios tour with my grandfather—I remember feeling like this was another means by which I could do magic."[17]

In fact, the day he and Kelvin visited Universal Studios was the day J.J. decided to dedicate his life to filmmaking. Abrams was so inspired that when he got home, he borrowed his parents' 8mm motion picture camera and attempted to make a stop-motion film using toy monsters. This was the start of his film career. "I had seen the makeup show and the stunt show, and I was blown away by the whole notion that movies were made by people and didn't just pop into being," he says. "I realized that making movies was an amazing way of experimenting and expressing myself, and I just kept doing it."[18]

J.J. Abrams visited the Universal Studios theme park in Hollywood, California (shown in 2007), when he was eight years old. The tour inspired him to dedicate his life to filmmaking.

J.J. Abrams's father, Gerald Abrams, had an office at Paramount Studios (seen here in 2013), where a young J.J. was able to wander the sets and watch various movies and TV shows being made.

On the Set

J.J. also got to visit Paramount Studios, where his father worked. The security guards knew the boy and let him wander around unchecked. He often snuck into the darkened sound stages, where he sat up in the bleachers watching the actors go over their lines. This deepened his desire to become part of their world. He recalls:

> My dad had an office at Paramount, and so when I was 11, 12 years old, I would go to the office with my father, and I would wander around the lot. I got to know the guards who were there, so they'd let me in and I'd sit in the empty bleachers and watch *Happy Days* or *Laverne and Shirley* or *Mork and Mindy*. I vividly remember seeing Robin Williams in civilian clothes, rehearsing and doing a bunch of crazy accents. I remember watching Ron Howard and Henry

Winkler and those guys, and it's a strange thing when you're a kid and there's The Fonz, such a hugely important part of your childhood. Yet you go to the set and see Henry Winkler, and in real life, he's nothing like The Fonz. It was disconcerting and confusing, but at the same time demystifying and fun.[19]

J.J. also often watched his father as he worked on one of his film productions. Always curious, J.J. asked Gerald lots of questions, and he absorbed everything that was going on around him. He watched with a purpose—to learn, so that he might duplicate what he saw in his home movies. He explains: "It was great just watching my father. I would go to sets with my dad, and just watching what he did, seeing how production really works, asking adults questions. . . . It's one of those things that fueled me. I'd been making Super 8 [8mm] films since I was 8 years old, and seeing how it was really done, even though I still didn't understand a lot of it, was something I could use."[20]

Creative Pastimes

When J.J. was not wandering Paramount Studios' back lot, he had a variety of hobbies that occupied his spare time. A poor athlete, he was often last to be chosen for sports and physical games. Lacking confidence in his physical abilities, he turned to other activities to fill his time. "I was definitely the fat kid making movies," he recalls. "I was the loner oddball kid who didn't have the confidence."[21]

To fill his time, he tinkered—building models, taking things apart, and transforming toys and household objects into more imaginative items. For instance, he carved out wooden blocks and painted them so that they resembled walkie-talkies, which he and Grunberg pretended to talk into. He also painted the outside of his computer to make it look like it was made of stone. He sculpted figurines out of clay, sketched, and wrote stories. He also played, composed, and recorded music. A lifelong music lover, he played keyboards and guitar and experimented with sound effects on a synthesizer. Making music still remains one of his favorite hobbies. He has his own recording studio, where he composes the theme songs for many of his television series.

He also used his recording equipment to record the prank phone calls he often made. But unlike most prank phone calls that typically revolve around a silly joke (like "Is your refrigerator running?"), his calls were based on detailed stories that he created. As his sister recalls, "I'd love to . . . tell you he did all these completely annoying, awful things. . . . But he was a good kid. The worst stuff he did was make crank calls with his friends. But even his crank calls were extraordinarily involved, in-depth things. There was always a story behind it."[22]

Other hobbies were going to the movies and watching television. According to his sister, J.J. watched about three hours of television each morning before going to school, and even more television when he arrived home. Although he was entertained by what he saw, his viewing seemed to have a larger objective. Like a sponge, he absorbed everything he saw, and he learned: what constitutes good acting; what makes characters endearing; how sounds and music affect the story; how stories are plotted; how costumes, makeup, and special effects enhance the production; and much more. Says Tracy, "Even as a kid, I felt like he was watching it with a purpose. He was watching all this stuff and taking in what he could and sort of needed."[23]

Favorite TV Shows

When it came to his viewing habits, he watched almost anything. But his favorite television shows have had a lasting impact on him. These featured mystery, emotion, and illusions. One of his favorite programs was *The Six Million Dollar Man*, which told the story of an astronaut with superhuman bionic body parts who worked for a secret government agency. The idea of combining technology and humanity fascinated J.J. He liked the concept so much that years later he featured it in his television series *Almost Human*.

The eerie science-fiction series *The Twilight Zone* was another of his favorites. Abrams ranks the series' creator, Rod Serling,

One of J.J. Abrams's favorite TV programs growing up was
The Six Million Dollar Man, starring Lee Majors (center)
and Farrah Fawcett (right). Its combination of technology
and humanity inspired some of Abrams's own TV programs.

among his personal heroes. Says Abrams: "He did my favorite thing—he took outlandish situations and told them through emotional characterization,"[24] which is something Abrams does in his own work.

He also liked watching old movies on television. An early version of *The Hunchback of Notre Dame* had a big effect on him.

I remember as a kid just being in absolute tears over the Charles Laughton Hunchback of Notre Dame I had seen on TV. . . .

It is literally this defining movie for me, and it just killed me. And the idea of this misunderstood, huge-hearted-

Rod Serling (seated)—one of Abrams's personal heroes— poses with actors on the set of a 1963 episode of his most famous TV show, **The Twilight Zone.**

seeming monster. . . . And it was the idea of that love story [that] was so profound. . . .

There's something about monsters that I think kids always, you know, are drawn to and curious about. I always loved that idea of combining that kind of emotion with something that was so . . . horrific or scary.[25]

Not surprisingly, many of J.J.'s home movies featured monsters, and years later he created a misunderstood monster in the film *Cloverfield*.

Although all his hobbies kept him quite busy, it was his newest hobby—making home movies—that began to preoccupy him. Many of his classmates called him a "geek" because of his fascination with seemingly oddball activities. At the time, being called a geek was meant as an insult, and it hurt J.J.'s feelings. But that has changed.

Today, geeks are considered cool people. This is largely due to the rise of technology, much of which was invented by people, like J.J., who did not always fit in. It also is due to the great popularity of movies about superheroes, technology, space, and fantasy worlds—subjects that were formerly considered silly or odd. Abrams, whose work has helped popularize these subjects and make them mainstream, has been dubbed the "King of the Geeks" by the media. But unlike when he was a child, J.J. embraces the title and his fans. As he explains,

The definition of "geek" has changed. When I started, a geek was an undeniable loser: long-necked, trips over his own feet, a complete outcast. And now "geek" means someone who likes science-fiction. When I was a kid, it was a huge insult to be a geek. Now it's a point of pride in a weird way. I feel very lucky to be working in a business and to be part of stories that are embraced by people who fit the current definition of geek.[26]

So, even though J.J.'s distinctive aptitudes and interests set him apart from most of his peers, these very things made him special. They are an important part of what he is noted for today. In fact, had he tried harder to fit in, he might not have become the man he is today. At eight years old, his experiments with his parents' motion picture camera were just beginning. What started as a childish hobby would soon become an obsession that would propel him toward a future that no one could imagine.

Chapter 2

Lights, Camera, Action!

J.J.'s experiments with his parents' movie camera increased his enthusiasm for movie making. He dreamed of owning his own camera, and he begged his grandfather to buy him one. He recalls:

> I would call him, and I'd be like, "Listen, Grandpa, I really need this camera. You don't understand. This is, like, you know, I want to make movies. . . ." And my grandmother was the greatest. Because she'd . . . get on the [other line and] be like, "Harry, it's better than the drugs. He should be doing—" She was fantastic.[27]

When he was about ten years old, his dream came true. His grandparents bought him a Super 8 camera. Then, a few years later they got him a synthesizer so that he could add sound effects to his films. Once he had his own camera, J.J.'s life revolved around making movies.

When J.J. was a boy, video cameras, smart phones, and other modern devices associated with homemade movies did not exist. Making movies with a Super 8 camera was a lot more complicated than making a video. J.J. could not just point and click. There was no instant viewing feature, no undo feature, no editing or musical apps; and there was no Internet where he could post his work. Eight-millimeter film came in a container, which J.J. loaded into the camera. Each cartridge produced about three minutes' worth of film and sound. Once J.J. used the film, he

As a young filmmaker, J.J. Abrams used a Super 8 camera—a common and accessible tool for non-professionals at the time.

mailed it away to be developed. Then he waited to get the film back so that he could view and edit his movie.

Making changes to the movie was not easy, either. He had to cut off unwanted sections of film by hand and then carefully splice the remaining film back together with clear tape. It was a big undertaking for a little boy. Few children his age could master it. But J.J. took to it with a passion. Looking back, he compares what he did to what young filmmakers can do today. As he explains,

> When I was a kid, it was pretty rare for kids to even have a camera and make movies, mostly because it was kind of a

hassle. It was kind of expensive and the tools were kind of hard to come by. But now, whether it's you or your friends or parents, everyone's got a camera now, either on your phone or just a regular camera. So in a weird way, making movies now is so much more common than it was when I was growing up. . . .

Like I said, when I was a kid, it was real difficult, the film couldn't be reused. Editing was a real pain. . . . Nowadays, you can find a camera anywhere. Editing stuff together, putting in music, doing dissolves, fades, and all these things—now so much is available. . . . And now with the Internet you can post your movies for the whole world to see so it's not just for your family or neighborhood.[28]

The Multitasker

J.J. did much more than just operate the camera and edit the film. For J.J., a good part of the fun of making movies was the secondary tasks, which provided a perfect outlet for his creativity. He wrote the scripts; made the props, costumes, scenery, and visual and sound effects; composed the score; cast the actors; and directed, filmed, and edited all of his projects. And, he frequently acted in his productions. He especially liked creating special effects. He made plaster masks, and he produced bloody open wounds on his characters using derma-wax, a special kind of soft wax that can be used on the skin. Oozing from the wounds was fake blood that he made with food coloring and corn syrup. He used his mother's makeup, too, to create gory effects. He laughingly recalls that "I would . . . ask my mom if I could borrow her makeup—which didn't trouble her because she knew I was going to basically just kill someone with it."[29]

No one and nothing was out of bounds. Once, he transformed his mother into a fire-breathing monster. "I made my mom into a creature—she smoked cigarettes for a year and this was luckily during that period of time—and I had her take a cigarette and I'd say, 'And . . . action!' and she'd have the smoke come up. And it was the worst, the dumbest thing ever, but to me it was *huge*—like 'Victory!'"[30]

A film splicer is a key tool for editing Super 8 and 16mm film. The film is physically cut, and the segments are then taped back together in the desired order.

J.J. created other monsters out of clay and built model airplanes, which he blew up on film. He constructed flying objects (which he hung from wires) that attacked his actors. Greg Grunberg remembers: "There was this one [movie] where this doll levitates and floats across the room and starts biting my neck. Even now, I ask him, 'How did you do that?'"[31]

Sometimes he would move furniture and cover the walls with paper to create a desired effect. As he recalls,

I had friends come over and . . . we'd make sets in rooms. Like, I'd take all the furniture out of my room and I would, you know, put, like, black crepe paper on the wall and, you know, all this crazy stuff. My parents would come home and all the furniture would be in the hallway and they'd be like, what [is] . . . going on here? You know, it was always like some ridiculous thing that we were doing. . . .

These were all just experiments of things to try and create an illusion of something that I wanted to do.[32]

Making a Major Motion Picture

It takes hundreds of people to make a major motion picture. Work begins before the movie even begins filming. The first stage is known as preproduction, which involves developing the script and hiring the actors and crew. The screenwriter, producer, and director lead the preproduction team.

The next stage is filming or production. It involves a large number of people besides the producer, director, and actors. There are a set decorating team, a props crew, a makeup team, a costume design team, an art department, a construction crew, and a painting crew. The filming is done by a camera crew, headed by a cinematographer. There are also a lighting crew, a sound department, a special-effects team, a transportation team, a catering/food team, and a publicity team.

When production is finished, postproduction or film editing begins. During postproduction, the director works with a film editor to edit the film. Sound effects, music, and visual effects are integrated into the film at this time. A postproduction supervisor coordinates the postproduction crew, which includes a large musical team, a large visual-effects team, a sound editing team, and a picture editing team.

Familiar Faces

To get actors for his productions, J.J. enlisted his family and friends. His sister, Tracy, like his pal Grunberg, was a frequent star. Since most of Abrams's movies involved chases, monsters, graphic fights, and murder, both of his stars usually met with gruesome fates. Tracy, especially, frequently played the role of a victim. "He would strangle her," Gerald Abrams recalls. "He would shoot her. He would have her jump off a roof. She got killed in more ways than you can imagine."[33]

As he got older, J.J. acquired a circle of friends who were also interested in filmmaking. He used all of them in his home movies. Interestingly, he still socializes and works with many of these individuals, including cinematographer Larry Fong and writer–producer–director Matt Reeves. Says Fong: "When you're a friend of J.J., it's kind of this weird club where you end up

Cinematographer Larry Fong is a longtime friend of J.J. Abrams's. They've been working together since their youth, when they started making home movies together.

seeing each other over the decades. . . . He hires you or you're part of his company and you stay there. It's kind of a family thing."[34]

J.J. readily admits that his early films were not very good. Mainly they involved chases, fights, murders, explosions, and monsters. At first, J.J. was more interested in experimenting and trying different visual effects than in telling stories. As he became more accomplished, he became more concerned with plots. He explains:

> The movies that I made were often just these sort of experiments to try to do things visually. . . . There was no precision. There was no easy way to do it. There were all sorts of stupid things that I would do, just tests like that to see if it would work. Years later I would start to tell stories with a little more of a narrative, with a beginning, middle, and end, and I'd use those kinds of techniques that over years I'd just been playing with for some kind of story effect.[35]

Fan Boy

Right from the start, J.J. took his movie making quite seriously. He thought of it more as a job than a hobby. And, he was motivated to do whatever it took to do his job well. He says:

> It was like the dream job. . . . To get to use my dad's camera—or, later, when my grandfather bought me my own, was incredibly fortunate. I started making movies when I was 8, so to be 11 or 12 or 15, or whatever, and to be making movies for half your lifetime! I remember being in high school, and doing these movies, and it really was a lifesaver. It let me escape into some kind of other place and gave me a sense of purpose. And that's pretty much how I still feel, which is that I get to . . . work on movies and stories that I can sort of lose myself in.[36]

Because many of his films were modeled after horror movies, J.J. poured over magazines such as *Fangoria*, *Cinefex*, and *CINE-MAGIC*. Geared toward amateur filmmakers of horror movies, these magazines provided step-by-step instructions in film-making and visual-effects techniques. They featured articles by legendary special-effects artists and film directors such as Dick Smith and Don Dohler, among others. J.J. was not shy about reaching out to these men for advice. He sent them fan letters in which he asked them all sorts of technical questions. They were quick to reply. And, over time, he developed relationships with them by writing these letters. Special-effects master Dick Smith even sent J.J. a sample of his work. Abrams recalls:

> I think I was 12, maybe I was 14, and I got, I came home one day and there was a box, a little teeny box. . . . I opened up the box and [there] was a tongue in the box. . . .

Special effects makeup artist Dick Smith creates a mask form for an actor. Abrams reached out to technical experts such as Smith for advice as a young filmmaker.

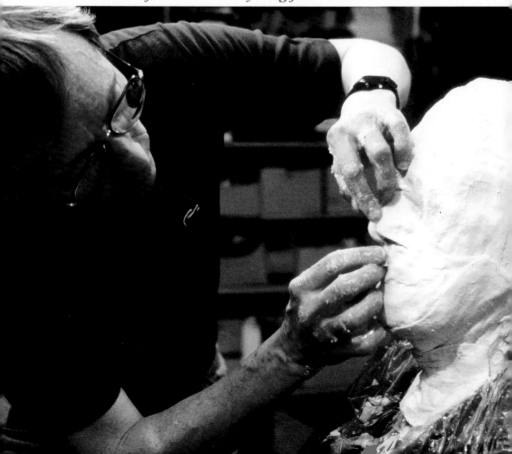

And it was from *The Exorcist*, which he had done. . . . He had this little handwritten note, I still have it, that said, "Put a little dab of peanut butter in the tongue and it will stick [to the wearer's own tongue]." . . . It was what Linda Blair [lead actor in *The Exorcist*] wore in one of the scenes where she had to stick her tongue out. It had to be like, you know, four or five inches longer [than Blair's actual tongue]. And my mom came home and she was like, what's that? I'm like, oh, it's just a tongue that Dick Smith, you know. . . . She's like, what man sent you a tongue? What's going on?

It didn't seem like a good thing for her kid to be doing.[37]

Meeting Other Heroes

J.J. also spent a lot of time going to the movies. He went because he loved movies and wanted to learn from some of the talented filmmakers of his time. His favorite movies included romantic comedies, horror and science-fiction films, and anything directed by his two favorite directors—Steven Spielberg, whose films include *E.T. the Extra-Terrestrial*, *Jaws*, and *Jurassic Park*, and John Carpenter, whose films include *Escape from New York*, *Halloween*, and *The Fog*.

When J.J. was a teenager, he got to meet Carpenter at an early screening of *Escape from New York*. In an effort to improve the film, which was still in its early stage, Carpenter invited a small group of people to view it. J.J.'s father was among the guests, and he took J.J. along. After showing the film, Carpenter asked the group for their comments. When Gerald Abrams suggested cutting the opening scene of the film, J.J. thought he would die of embarrassment. How could his dad criticize his hero? But as he watched Carpenter carefully take notes, he realized that even great artists do whatever it takes to make their work better. "What I learned . . . just by watching him [was to] be open to criticism. . . . He knew he had a movie that at the time was problematic in certain ways and he was trying to fix it."[38]

That realization gave J.J. the courage to make a comment, too. After all, maybe his comment could help Carpenter. J.J. said that

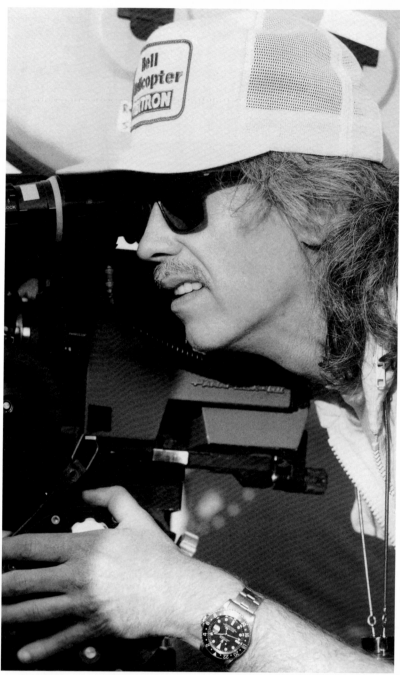

John Carpenter directs a scene on set in 1988. Carpenter is among J.J. Abrams's favorite movie directors.

Don Dohler

As a youth, J.J. Abrams maintained a correspondence with Don Dohler, who is best known as a filmmaker of low-budget horror and science-fiction movies. Between 1976 and 2006, Dohler created a total of eleven movies, most of which he wrote, directed, filmed, and produced in and around his home in Baltimore, Maryland. His films were gory stories featuring decapitations, psycho killers, organ-harvesting aliens, zombies, murderous housewives, chases through dark forests, and gallons of fake blood and fog.

In addition to making films, Dohler published a number of magazines. He started his first publication, which he modeled after *MAD Magazine*, when he was fifteen years old. It was called *WILD*. His next magazine, *CINEMAGIC*, which he started in the 1960s, targeted amateur filmmakers. It featured interviews with industry professionals and step-by-step instructions on filmmaking techniques. In 1993, he created another magazine, *Movie Club*, which celebrated classic horror movies of the 1950s.

Dohler, who had a large international fan base, died of cancer in 2006 at age sixty. A documentary film about his life was released in 2009.

---

it was unclear whether or not a character survived a car crash. When the movie was released, J.J. was surprised to see that Carpenter had cut the opening scene, as Gerald had suggested, and he had added a shot of the crash victim's dead body. The fact that Carpenter had taken his suggestion seriously had a big effect on J.J. He realized that his opinion mattered. Since then, when he feels strongly about something, he does not hesitate to speak his mind.

When J.J. could not go to the theater to see a movie, he listened to the sound track and imagined what was happening on screen. He recalls: "I used to go to a secondhand record store . . .

J.J. Abrams composed and recorded the score for the low-budget film Nightbeast *using a reel-to-reel tape deck.*

and buy soundtracks that had a composer I liked, even when I hadn't seen the film or had any idea what the story was about. I'd go home, put my headphones on, lie on my floor, and listen to them, just looking at the artwork or reading the liner notes, and imagine what the movie was about."[39]

Listening to movie scores also gave J.J. ideas for the scores and sound effects he composed for his own movies. When he was sixteen years old, he was offered the chance to compose the score for *Nightbeast*, a horror film directed by Dohler. In the course of their correspondence, J.J. mentioned that he composed the music and sound effects for his home movies. Dohler, who operated on an extremely low budget, offered the boy the chance to compose the score for *Nightbeast*. Says Abrams:

> It was such a crazy thrill to be asked to be involved in one of his movies. I would watch a scene that Don Dohler sent me and I would time it with a watch and write down where things would happen. And then I'd go upstairs, and I would use whatever instrument I could use. I had a little porta-studio, a four-track thing or a reel-to-reel tape deck. It was just the most preposterous set-up and I would send him back music, some of which he used in the movie.
>
> It was just a very exciting thing, to be involved in a movie on any level.[40]

Festival of "The Best Teen Super 8mm Films of '81"

All of J.J.'s hard work was starting to pay off. Through his studies and experiments, he learned a lot about cinematography, screenwriting, and visual and sound effects. However, on one occasion his growing skill as a filmmaker got him into trouble. He filmed a fight scene in a parking garage in which it appeared that a character got flipped over the fifth-floor railing and was barely hanging on. Abrams was editing the scene in his bedroom when his father walked in, saw the film, and exploded. He was angry at J.J. for risking his friend's life to make a movie.

In reality, the character dangling from the railing was a dummy that J.J. had made and that he rigged with wires so the legs kicked. Although J.J. did not like making his father upset, he was thrilled that the scene looked so real that it fooled Gerald. As he explains:

> It was the greatest victory. . . . I was just so happy that he believed it, and it literally just speaks to that desperate desire as, like, a little fat magician kid . . . wanting . . . your family to believe that that little . . . foam yellow rabbit just

disappeared from your hand or whatever. . . . It's that same thing . . . all you want is for people to believe it.[41]

Most of the time, J.J.'s increasing ability as a filmmaker did not lead to trouble. In fact, it helped him gain a place in a film festival that featured the work of teen filmmakers. Fifteen-year-old J.J. often watched a public-access television show that spotlighted the work of adult amateur filmmakers. J.J. thought his work should be shown on the program, so he called the show's host, Gerard Ravel, and introduced himself. Ravel arranged to meet J.J. and view his work. He was so impressed that he interviewed Abrams on camera and aired one of his films. Once J.J. appeared on the program, other young filmmakers started calling in, too. In fact, the response was so overwhelming that Ravel decided to organize a film festival featuring the work of Abrams and other young filmmakers. He called the festival "The Best Teen Super 8mm Films of '81." Ravel recalls:

One day, I get a message on my phone machine. It said, "My name is J.J. I'm 15 years old. I've been making films for seven years, and I would like to be on your show." I thought it was a prank . . . because most of my audience was older. So I called the number and I went over to his home . . . and met him and his parents. They were really nice people and J.J. was one of the most polite, courteous kids I ever met. He loved working with makeup and special effects. He put the films on his Super 8 projector, and I knew this kid was going to make it. His enthusiasm was over the top, and as soon as I saw him, I said, "You know what? He's going to be a great interview. He's going to inspire other people to call my show." . . . Then the next week I get another call, and it's Matt Reeves. He says, "I'm 15 years old. I saw J.J.'s films on your show. I have a 30-minute film and I'd like to be on your show." That's when I knew I'd struck a chord, because now all of these kids who were wanting to be filmmakers were watching my show. . . .
    After Matt and J.J. were on, then we said, "What if we did a show at the Nuart Theater [an art house cinema in West Los Angeles]?," and they both were enthusiastic.[42]

The festival was a huge success. It helped launch the careers of many film industry greats. Although it would be a few years before J.J. joined their ranks, J.J.'s participation in the festival had far-reaching and unexpected consequences.

Chapter 3

The Professional

Having his work shown in the film festival put fifteen-year-old J.J. in the spotlight. A review of the festival in the *Los Angeles Times* raved about J.J.'s film *High Voltage* and featured an interview with J.J. and his friend Matt Reeves. In the interview, J.J. mentioned that he wanted to make movies like filmmaker Steven Spielberg someday. As luck would have it, the article caught Spielberg's eye and piqued his interest in the young moviemaker.

Like J.J., Spielberg spent much of his youth making 8mm films. By this time, these early Spielberg films were cracked with age and in serious need of cleaning and repair. Considered invaluable by the art world, the films were the only copies of the filmmaker's earliest work. Typically, reels of valuable fragile film are repaired by a professional film archivist, not inexperienced teenagers. But upon reading the *Los Angeles Times* article, Spielberg had his assistant contact J.J. and offer him and Reeves a job repairing the films. "It was insane," said Abrams. "It was like giving us the Mona Lisa and saying, 'Will you clean this?'"[43]

Spielberg has never explained why he gave the job to the teenagers. It might have been because he saw a bit of his younger self in them. For whatever reason, Spielberg trusted the boys. They eagerly accepted the job, for which they were paid a total of three hundred dollars. Not everyone was as confident that the boys would succeed as Spielberg. At one point, J.J.'s mom walked into his bedroom and panicked when she saw yards of

Steven Spielberg (pictured with the E.T. puppet in 1980) is one of J.J. Abrams's heroes. Spielberg also gave a young Abrams the job of cleaning and restoring his early 8mm films.

Steven Spielberg

Steven Spielberg is one of J.J. Abrams's favorite filmmakers. Spielberg was born in 1946 and grew up in Arizona. He started making movies when he was twelve, to earn a Boy Scout merit badge. When his parents divorced, he moved to California with his father. He unsuccessfully tried to get into the University of Southern California's film school. After being rejected twice, he attended California State University, Long Beach. He dropped out but went back to school and finished his degree in 2002, thirty-five years after he originally started college.

Spielberg worked as an unpaid intern at Universal Studios in the 1960s. As an intern he made his first short film for commercial release, *Amblin*, in 1968. He later named his production company Amblin, after the film. Universal then hired him to direct different episodes of various television series and made-for-TV movies. His directed his first full-length motion picture, *The Sugarland Express*, in 1974. His next film, *Jaws*, made Spielberg famous. Some of his other films include *Close Encounters of the Third Kind*, *Raiders of the Lost Ark*, *E.T. the Extra-Terrestrial*, *Poltergeist*, *The Goonies*, *The Color Purple*, *Jurassic Park*, and *Schindler's List*.

unrolled film strewn all over the floor. "'What have you done?!?' she remembered screaming. 'He's going to sue us! We're going to lose our house! We're going to lose our cars!'"[44]

That did not happen. J.J. and Reeves loved restoring the films and did a good job. They especially enjoyed getting a glimpse of Spielberg's early work. It surprised J.J. to see the similarities between his own films and that of the master. It made him feel closer to Spielberg, whom he would not actually meet until years later. He recalls:

> It was weird to see that his movies were as rough as mine in a way and as rough as my friend's in a way. It was heart-

ening and also somehow scary. . . . It gave me this bizarre
sense of connection to a man whose work I loved.[45]

On to College

Abrams continued making movies all through high school. He
also composed music; wrote a novel, short stories, and screenplays; and starred in a high school production of *Fiddler on
the Roof*. Because he had excellent grades and his family was
well-off financially, upon his graduation from Palisades Charter
High School in 1984, he could attend almost any college he
wanted. He planned to go to the University of Southern California to study filmmaking, except that his father steered him
in a different direction. A successful movie producer in his own
right, Gerald Abrams knew what it takes to succeed in the film

*Students lounge and study on the campus of Sarah
Lawrence College—one of the most expensive schools in
the country—in Bronxville, New York. Abrams chose to
attend the liberal arts college after his father dissuaded
him from going to film school.*

industry. He advised his son that learning how to make films was not enough. He needed to learn more about people and the world in order to make believable films. A strong liberal arts education would provide him with the knowledge he needed to succeed in the film industry.

Taking his father's words to heart, Abrams investigated different liberal arts colleges. He was especially impressed with Sarah Lawrence College. "I heard about Sarah Lawrence," Abrams recalls. "It was a smaller, liberal arts college that encouraged independence and creativity, a half hour from Manhattan. It sounded like a dream. I went and visited the campus, and ended up going [to college] 3,000 miles from home."[46]

It proved to be an excellent choice. Abrams majored in English and history and spent most of his college career writing. He completed nine screenplays, a novel, and many short stories. Looking back on that work, he readily admits that much of it was not very good. But just as his skill as a filmmaker improved with practice, so did his skill as a writer. He explains:

> There were so many things that I wrote [in college]. . . . A lot of them were either abnormally pretentious attempts at modernizing things like *Anna Karenina*, or doing things like writing a kind of wannabe *Less than Zero* novel about kids who are always trying to find the great party, that's always kind of one party away. But each time I wrote something, I learned something, and it's actually made writing the next thing a little more comfortable.[47]

Taking writing classes with a special professor, Joe Papaleo, also helped Abrams grow as a writer. Papaleo was an award-winning novelist and academic who took a special interest in Abrams. The two spent hours in Papaleo's office going over Abrams's work. Papaleo made Abrams feel that what he had to say in his writing mattered. Giving a speech in 2010, as part of the TEACH campaign of the U.S. Department of Education, Abrams paid tribute to Papaleo, saying that Papaleo gave him the confidence he needed to succeed. "Before Joe Papaleo," Abrams explained, "I was a guy who wrote. But after Joe, I was a writer."[48]

Being around other students, especially female students, influenced Abrams as a writer, too. Sarah Lawrence began as a college for women. Although it became coed long before Abrams enrolled, it still had a high ratio of female-to-male students. Abrams spent a lot of time around women while at Sarah Lawrence. In fact, there were occasions in which he was the only man in a room filled with women. During these times he was largely ignored, giving him the opportunity to listen to their conversations and observe their body language. As a result he became more aware of how women interact with each other. It also gave him a better understanding of the opposite sex, which carried over into his writing.

Selling the First Screenplay

With only one semester left until he graduated, Abrams began to worry about the future. He had his heart set on following his dreams and pursuing a career in filmmaking. But getting a job in the entertainment industry was (and still is) highly competitive. His father could have helped him get a job as an assistant, but Abrams wanted to write, direct, or produce films. And, he wanted to make his way on his own ability.

Back in California during winter break of his senior year, Abrams ran into Jill Mazursky at a shopping mall. She was an acquaintance of Abrams's, and the daughter of film director Paul Mazursky. Like Abrams, she was trying to break into the film industry. Mazursky told J.J. about an idea she had for a screenplay. After a brainstorming session, the pair agreed to cowrite the script, which they called *Taking Care of Business*. It was a comedy about a businessman who loses his daily planner and the convict who finds it. Abrams and Mazursky sold the screenplay to Disney in 1988, right before Abrams graduated from Sarah Lawrence. The film, which was released in 1990, got mixed reviews. But as far as Abrams was concerned, it was all good.

Selling the screenplay was Abrams's ticket into the film industry. It launched his professional career and opened many doors for him. As he explains:

Actor Charles Grodin rides in a convertible in a scene from the 1990 film Taking Care of Business, *based on Abrams's first professional screenplay, co-written with Jill Mazursky.*

I owe everything I have to Jill. . . . She, like, totally made my career. . . . In my senior year at Sarah Lawrence, I came home for Christmas vacation and I was wandering around the mall, wondering what I was going to do when I graduated. . . . On my way down the escalator, in the mall that day, I saw Jill. . . . She told me about this idea she had for a script, about a guy—someone who's just working his way up in the corporate world—who loses his Filofax [a small notebook for writing dates and notes]. And I thought that the guy who found it should be this really tough guy who had just escaped from jail, like a tough Hispanic guy. Then we wrote a treatment for *Taking Care of Business*, and Jeffrey Katzenberg [the head of Disney's motion picture division at that time] bought it! . . .

Of course, they changed the whole thing. . . . It was still a great experience, and it gave me time and money to write more scripts.[49]

J.J. Abrams, Screenwriter

As of 2014, J.J. Abrams is credited with writing and/or creating a total of seventy-one films, episodes of television series, and video games. His work includes:

Star Wars: Episode VII—film screenplay
Joy Ride 3—film based on the characters created by Abrams
Fringe—television series created by Abrams, writer of six episodes
Undercovers—television series created by Abrams, writer of three episodes
Super 8—film screenplay
Lost—television series created by Abrams, writer of six episodes
Joy Ride 2: Dead Ahead—film based on the characters created by Abrams
Lost: Via Domus—video game creator
Lost: Missing Pieces—television miniseries, one episode
Avatar: The Last Airbender—television series, one episode
Alias—television series created by Abrams, writer of thirteen episodes
Mission: Impossible III—film screenplay
The Catch—creator of television series that was not aired
Alias—video game creator
Felicity—television series created by Abrams, writer of seventeen episodes
Joy Ride—film screenplay
Armageddon—film screenplay
Gone Fishing—film screenplay
Forever Young—film screenplay
Regarding Henry—film screenplay
Taking Care of Business—film screenplay

A String of Successes

The money Abrams earned from *Taking Care of Business* allowed him to move back to California after he graduated from Sarah

Lawrence in 1988 and to pursue his dreams. For the next two years, he shared an apartment with Greg Grunberg. The old friends had a lot of fun together. One of their favorite activities was playing video games. But Abrams never took his eye off the prize. He spent most of the time writing. He says that even when he, Grunberg, and his other old friends went out on the town, he could not take his mind off his work. More often than not, he would slip away so that he could go home to write.

He came up with the idea for a drama called *Regarding Henry* about an arrogant, unethical attorney who survives a bullet to the head during a robbery. As the lawyer struggles to heal, he becomes a better person. The finished screenplay aroused the interest of some of Hollywood's heaviest hitters: producer Scott Rudin, director Mike Nichols, and actor Harrison Ford. The trio loved the screenplay and vowed to make the movie. Their involvement almost guaranteed that the film would be a success. When Abrams's agent called to tell him, Abrams could not believe his ears. He explains: "Scott Rudin had read it, and he'd given it to Mike Nichols, who'd given it to Harrison Ford, and they were all going to make this movie. . . . It was literally the most preposterous phone call in the history of time. I didn't stop laughing for two weeks."[50]

Abrams spent a lot of time on the set watching the movie being made. He even played a bit part in the film. More importantly, because *Regarding Henry* involved some of Hollywood's biggest names, a screenplay by J.J. Abrams was now considered a hot property. That is one reason why he was paid 2 million dollars by Warner Brothers for his next creation, *Forever Young*, the largest amount ever paid for a screenplay at that time. It was a romantic drama based on one of Abrams's short stories. The film, which was released in 1992, was a box office hit, adding to the demand for Abrams's work.

Abrams bought a house and a sports car with some of his newly earned wealth. He had enough money left over to relax for a while, but he kept working. In the next few years, he directed a Japanese soda commercial; produced *The Pallbearer*, a romantic comedy written and directed by his friend Matt Reeves; cowrote *Going Fishing* with Mazursky; and took a small acting

Abrams was paid a then-record $2 million for the screenplay of Forever Young, *a 1992 film starring Mel Gibson (left) and Elijah Wood.*

part in the drama *Six Degrees of Separation*. And if all this was not enough to keep him busy, he worked as a script doctor. A script doctor is a writer who is hired to fix specific problems in an existing script, usually before the film goes into production. Abrams proved to be such an accomplished script doctor that he had more work than he could handle.

Although script doctors are not usually credited for their work, Abrams received writing credit for one of the screenplays he was hired to amend. The film was the 1998 blockbuster *Armageddon*. The film was panned by critics largely for its complete disregard for physics. Abrams was nominated for a Golden Raspberry (Razzie) award for the worst writing of a movie. That did not upset Abrams:

> I loved working on *Armageddon*, because it was insane. It was the craziest idea ever, and I remember working with a NASA scientist . . . and getting from him notes that were absolutely critical of the insane possibility of the physics

of the script. When I went back to [*Armageddon* producer] Jerry Bruckheimer and said, "Listen, there's no atmosphere or gravity on an asteroid," and I went through this list of things, and Jerry was like, "Yeah, we're keeping all that," I just thought, "You know what? This is just going to be a great roller coaster ride. It's not going to be a course in astrophysics." The movie, I think, was an incredibly fun ride.[51]

The public agreed with Abrams. The film was a huge commercial success, grossing over 200 million dollars in the United

States and spawning a novel based on the film and a theme park ride in Disneyland Paris. Plus, it proved that Abrams could write blockbuster action films.

Love and Marriage

Besides doing well professionally, Abrams's personal life, too, was on the upswing. In 1994, on a trip to New York City, he met a special woman named Katie McGrath. Abrams and a date went to a large dinner party that McGrath also attended. McGrath was a tall, attractive public relations executive who grew up in Maine and lived in New York. Abrams was struck by her beauty and introduced himself. She recalls: "He was actually on a date with someone else. . . . As the evening wore on, everyone sort of switched seats and he ended up sitting next to me —he has a whole story of the ruse he created in order for that to happen. But he was very funny. I mean, clever and funny."[52]

When the party ended, Abrams made up an excuse about having to go in the same direction as McGrath was going and the opposite direction of his date so that he could share a taxi with McGrath.

Steve Buscemi, Will Patton, Bruce Willis, Michael Clarke Duncan, Ben Affleck, and Owen Wilson (left to right) act in a scene from the 1998 film Armageddon, *on which Abrams worked as a script doctor.*

Abrams and his wife, Katie McGrath, arrive at the premiere of Star Trek *in Los Angeles, California, in April 2009. The couple met in 1994 and married two years later.*

On the surface, McGrath and Abrams were quite different. She was Catholic and he was Jewish; she worked in the corporate world, and he worked in movies. But despite their differences, they fell in love. For the next two years, they maintained a long-distance relationship. The two married in 1996, and Abrams moved to New York. The newlyweds lived in McGrath's apartment. She went to work each morning, while Abrams stayed home. It was not uncommon for her to find him still in his pajamas busily writing when she returned home in the evening.

Abrams and McGrath soon started a family and moved to California. Their son Henry was born in 1998; Gracie came along a year later, and their son August was born in 2006. Abrams is a devoted family man who could not be happier. "I'm married to the love of my life," he says, "and I have three kids who are the result of that love."[53]

Abrams says that his family is the most important thing in his life. He proves it by his dedication to them. He tries to spend as much time as possible with his children. He bathed them every night when they were small. Now that the children are older, he usually makes them breakfast every morning and drives them to school. Just as his grandfather built things with him, Abrams builds things with his children. He also makes greeting cards with them on his letterpress and helps them sculpt clay monsters similar to those he made as a child. He and the children create board games that the whole family plays. Abrams tries not to work late or on weekends, allowing him to spend time with his family. In fact, he has a film-editing room in his home so that he can work at home rather than put in late nights at the studio. Abrams also does chores around the house. He is very handy and frequently repairs anything that breaks around the house. And, of course, his family is a perfect audience for his magic tricks.

The Need for Secrecy

Although Abrams's life seemed to be perfect, he grew tired of fixing other people's scripts. So, when he was offered the opportunity to write an original screenplay for a new Superman movie in 2002, he got right to work. However, when a rough draft of a script titled *Superman: Flyby* was leaked online, major problems occurred. A reviewer on a popular website slammed the script, calling it "a disaster of epic proportions."[54]

The review caused a negative buzz among Superman fans, and the movie was never made. The incident greatly affected Abrams. "To have a script that is nowhere near the latest draft, let alone the final draft, being reviewed online, it frankly made me a little bit paranoid,"[55] he admits. Ever since that episode, he has maintained extremely tight security over all his projects. In fact, he is famous for the secrecy surrounding his creations.

Although *Superman: Flyby* was never made, on the whole, after graduating from college Abrams met with almost unprecedented success. Hollywood's fix-it man had become a millionaire before he was thirty. Now, he was eager to turn his attention to his own projects.

Chapter 4

TV Dynamo

Bored with fixing other people's screenplays and unhappy about what happened with *Superman*, Abrams turned his attention to the small screen. Before cable television made it popular for filmmakers to work in television, success in Hollywood was mainly measured by a person's work in films. In fact, few screenwriters voluntarily switched to writing for television. Abrams was the exception. He thought that working in television would allow him to be more creative. As he explains in a videotaped interview:

> The great thing about television, it's all about open-endedness, it's all about the evolution of a story. . . . There is no one who knows exactly how the end of a series is going to play when they write the pilot . . . so I think that television allows for a more kind of free-flowing creativity, whereas films by their nature require a more disciplined storytelling . . . so for that reason I think television . . . is a more freeing form.[56]

To help finance his foray into television, in 1998 Abrams established a film and television production company called Bad Robot with an old friend named Bryan Burk. A production company gets funds for television shows, films, or other artistic projects. It sets the budget for the projects and makes decisions on the selection of the director and actors.

Bad Robot

The offices of Bad Robot are a reflection of J.J. Abrams's interests, personality, and love of illusion. The offices are hard to find. There is no Bad Robot sign on the building that houses the production company. Instead, a big sign on the front of the building says "National Typewriter Company." This is not because the building was the former home of the typewriter company but because Abrams likes typewriters and misdirection. To get inside, visitors ring a doorbell that glows with an eerie green light. Next to the doorbell is a small sign that says "Are you ready?"

Inside, the building is a fun place with floating staircases, glass walls, movie memorabilia, common areas, and busy, busy people. Abrams's own office is on the second floor. On his desk is a telephone with no digits. To access the bathroom in Abrams's office, visitors must tug on a book about magic. Then, the wall opens and the bathroom is exposed.

There is a large roof-patio where parties are held. The building also houses recording studios, film-editing studios, a prop-making shop, a screening room, and a movie set. At any one time, multiple projects are being worked on, and secrecy is always maintained.

Bad Robot is pure Abrams. The building is filled with posters of his favorite movies, costumes and movie memorabilia, toy monsters and masks, and old-fashioned gadgets. His sister describes Abrams's office as "a glorified version of his bedroom growing up."[57] The company's name and logo, too, reflect Abrams's passions. He named the company Bad Robot because he has always been fascinated with robots, and he designed the company's logo using the voices of his son Henry and daughter, Gracie, saying "Bad Robot" into his computer as part of the company's end credits. As chief executive officer of the company,

Abrams has proved to be a shrewd businessman and made the company a huge success.

Strong Young Women

With Bad Robot established, Abrams began his first venture into television with a coming-of-age drama called *Felicity*, about a young woman who follows her high school crush to a college in New York City. Abrams created the series with Matt Reeves and cast Greg Grunberg in a leading role. Besides creating the series, Abrams composed the theme, was the executive producer, and wrote some of the episodes. Abrams got the idea for the series from an incident that happened to him in high school.

There was a shy girl in his class who was a gifted artist. Abrams approached her on graduation day and told her he admired her work. His comment made her very happy. Although he and the girl never communicated again, the incident gave J.J. the idea for a story about two people who meet at the end of high school and are drawn to each other romantically. As he explains, "The idea for *Felicity* was really something that I thought about for a while. I loved the idea of a character who was such a romantic that she would follow this crazy sort of capricious whim and change her whole educational plan. The thing I loved about her had nothing to do with her gender. It was her romanticism."[58]

The show was a hit. In fact, *Time* magazine named it one of the top one hundred television series of all time. One of its most unique features was that the main character was a strong young woman. While this was not common when the show first aired, in 1998, strong women protagonists would become a hallmark of Abrams's work. Other elements of the series were less characteristic of Abrams's work. *Felicity* was sweeter and more romantic than much of Abrams's later, more mysterious work. But the last five episodes, which feature a time travel arc, and an episode honoring *The Twilight Zone* foreshadowed the type of stories J.J. would become famous for.

While working on *Felicity*, Abrams came up with an idea for another television series called *Alias*, about a young woman who leads the double life of a graduate student/spy. Abrams first

Keri Russell holds her 1999 Golden Globe Award for best actress for her work on Felicity, *Abrams's first venture into television.*

came up with the idea in jest. He was at a writers' meeting for *Felicity* and was having trouble coming up with ideas for an episode. As a joke, he said that it would be much easier to come up with stories if *Felicity* were secretly a spy. A short time later, ABC told him they wanted to make a new series with a young female lead. Abrams told them about his spy idea, and they asked him to write a pilot.

The network liked the pilot so much that they not only decided to air the series but also hired Abrams to be the director. Abrams had not directed a major project since he graduated from college. The opportunity to direct *Alias* was a dream come true. It gave Abrams control of something he created, from start to finish. As he explains,

> Directing's the best. . . .Whenever I've directed something, there's this feeling of demand and focus that I like.

Jennifer Garner and Michael Vartan act in a scene from Alias in 2001. Abrams's second television production was a great success and ran for five years.

And secondly, it means that you've gotten through all the writing stuff, and the producing stuff, and casting, and prep, and all those stages that are seemingly endless. So directing is sort of the reward for all the work you put in before. And then there's the editing, which is another amazing stage of the process. It's incredible, the moments you can create.[59]

The plot of the series depended heavily on mystery and illusion, and Abrams loved it. The public, too, loved it. The series, which featured Grunberg and Jennifer Garner in the cast and helped turn Garner into a star, ran for five years and was a huge success. It acquired a large fan following. And it established Abrams as a master of multiple genres.

Creating a Cultural Phenomenon

Abrams's next creation was a science-fiction series called *Lost* that had a big impact on popular culture and made Abrams famous. *Lost* told the story of a group of airplane crash survivors stranded on a weird and mysterious island. Originally, ABC had wanted to de-

The cast of Lost *poses at the TV show's 2004 premiere in Honolulu, Hawaii. The series' success established Bad Robot as a powerful production company.*

velop a television series based on the movie *The Castaway*, about a group of people on a deserted island. But they had trouble coming up with an actual story, so they turned to Abrams. Says actor-writer-producer Thom Sherman, "Anytime we had an idea at ABC that we were having troubles with, the first name that would always pop up in our heads was, 'What would J.J. do with it?'"[60]

Abrams came up with an interesting idea. He explains:

I started thinking about what a story would be, that would be interesting to me about a plane crash and the survivors

J.J. Abrams Trivia

Want to know more about J.J. Abrams? Here are some facts:

His astrological sign is Cancer.

His favorite character that he created is Sydney Bristow of the television show *Alias*—favorite because she is sweet and brave.

His favorite writers are Mark Twain, H.G. Wells, and Stephen King.

He is 5 feet 7 inches tall. His wife is a half inch taller than he is.

His favorite graphic novelist is Chris Ware.

He is a big fan of the television series *Downton Abbey*.

His hair is naturally curly.

In college, he used the screenplay for *Ordinary People* by Alvin Sargent as a guide for writing screenplays.

He says that the fictional drink Slusho tastes overly sweet and blue.

Many of his television programs and films revolve around groups of people who come together to meet a challenge.

He has a recurring nightmare about being in a plane crash.

His directing-debut film, *Mission: Impossible III*, was the most expensive film ever made by a first-time director.

His net worth is estimated at 95 million dollars.

He directed an episode of the television comedy series *The Office*.

He designs T-shirts for fun.

His favorite food is a turkey, cranberry, and cole slaw sandwich.

He has a collection of small tin robots.

He likes to paint and sculpt.

of a plane crash. . . . Then I had this one idea, which was: What if the island wasn't just an island . . . and what if . . . they found a hatch [a door in the ground that led to a mysterious underground room] on the island. . . . And this weird little thing, for me, was a nugget . . . that could be kind of cool.[61]

ABC liked Abrams's idea and asked him to write the pilot episode. But Abrams was too busy with *Alias* to write the pilot on his own. He needed someone to help him. ABC suggested the young writer named Damon Lindelof. The two immediately hit it off. In only five days, they wrote an outline for the series' pilot. It was so compelling that ABC committed to making the show without ever seeing a script.

The series, which premiered in 2004 and ran for six seasons, was a cultural phenomenon. The complex mysteries that surrounded the island and the characters spawned an elaborate mythology and devoted fans who called themselves "Losties." Websites appeared where Losties speculated about the island's and the survivors' secrets and posted fan fiction. Interest in the show was so great that ABC launched a variety of cross-media activities for fans, some of which were new concepts, such as podcasts and alternate-reality games.

Abrams served as the series creator, executive producer, theme music composer, opening logo designer, and writer and director of some episodes. Although his involvement diminished considerably after the first season, the series, in which ordinary people faced extraordinary events involving monsters, illusions, and mysteries, had Abrams's fingerprints all over it. Its success firmly established Bad Robot as a powerful production company, and Abrams as a creative mastermind.

Movie Director

Abrams's success in television put his work in such high demand that he was forced to turn down many interesting projects. One of these was writing the screenplay for *War of the Worlds*, a big-budget film directed by Steven Spielberg and starring

Tom Cruise, the well-known actor and producer. Abrams and Spielberg had met a few years earlier, but Abrams had never gotten over being in awe of the older man. Abrams had never met Cruise until Spielberg introduced them. Abrams worried that turning down two such famous and powerful men would hurt his career, but he had no choice. He was just too busy. He describes what happened:

> I got a call that Steven Spielberg, Tom Cruise, and Paula Wagner [Cruise's longtime producing partner] wanted to come over for a meeting. . . . We had this two-hour meeting. I had known Steven for a few years, but it was always an out-of-body experience, and so to compound it with having Cruise on the same sofa, it was freaky. It was really fun, Tom and I got along great, [but] I couldn't do the movie because I was filming the *Lost* pilot. I felt like I had just committed career suicide.[62]

In reality, turning down the opportunity did not hurt Abrams's career. In fact, that meeting helped launch Abrams's career as a film director. During the meeting Cruise mentioned that he had never seen *Alias*, so Abrams gave him a DVD of the first two seasons of the series. Cruise went home, watched the first episode, and was hooked. He loved Abrams's work. He wanted to make a film with Abrams, and even though Abrams had no experience as a film director, he wanted Abrams to direct. So, when the person scheduled to direct Cruise's next movie, *Mission: Impossible III*, quit, Cruise, who was starring in and producing the film, offered the job to Abrams. Once again, Abrams had too much work to take the job. In order to get Abrams on board, Cruise delayed the release of the movie by two years just to accommodate Abrams's schedule.

Although Abrams hired on as the director, he wound up rewriting the script with the help of his writing partners on *Alias*, Roberto Orci and Alex Kurtzman. The original script did not mesh with Abrams's ideas about storytelling. He felt the main character needed to be developed more so that the audience would root for him. He explains:

I really liked the original script, but it was not something I could deliver. It was like, I love the Bible, but I couldn't have written that. . . . I wanted to do a movie that was about the home life, the truths a spy deals with. What's it like to come home to a partner who can't know what your job is? It's what got me excited about doing *Alias*—it's where the absolutely extra-ordinary, unexpected, and supersecret meets the absolutely mundane. . . .

This is a story about a man who's a spy, who's in love, who finds himself in a very desperate situation and has to reconcile these pieces of his life. We did not want this to be

Abrams directs actor Tom Cruise in a scene for **Mission Impossible III,** *the first Hollywood movie directed by Abrams.*

one of those movies that feel as if eight . . . action sequences were conceived and shoved into some kind of story to tie them together.[63]

Cruise was wise to put his faith in Abrams. The film got favorable reviews and was a box office hit. Directing it added another hyphen to Abrams's résumé: film director, the job he had dreamed of since he was a boy, and the job that he found he liked best of all. As he explains,

The opportunity to do this movie was so remarkable. I cannot think of anyone else who would let someone who never directed a feature before take the reins of something that is this large in scale, this expensive, and yet Tom [Cruise] did. I mean, he believed in me, and never wavered from that during the entire experience. I do think that there were moments that I was in shock that I was given this opportunity, but the truth is I wanted to do this all my life. . . . I did not necessarily think that the first movie I would get a chance to direct would be something as large as this one, but the crew was so incredible. Tom and his producing partner, Paula Wagner, were so supportive from the beginning that I always felt, and I believe the whole crew always felt, incredibly supported and safe, which always allows for more creativity. So the whole experience was great, and I honestly never doubted that I could do it. It actually felt incredibly comfortable doing it.[64]

Mysterious Viral Marketing

In the next few years, Abrams was involved in a number of projects, including a film called *Cloverfield*. Abrams came up with the idea for the film, then turned to a writer named Drew Goddard to write the screenplay. The film was modeled after the horror movies that Abrams loved as a boy, and it was directed by his friend Reeves. The film follows a group of New Yorkers on the night that a gigantic monster attacks the city. Abrams got the idea for the monster while promoting *Mission: Impossible III*

Michael Stahl-David, Matt Reeves, J.J. Abrams, Lizzy Caplan, and Drew Goddard (left to right) pose in front of a mock Statue of Liberty at the Japan premiere of Cloverfield in 2008.

in Japan. He explains: "I was in Japan with my son, and all he wanted to do is go to toy stores. And we saw all these Godzilla toys [The original *Godzilla* film was Japanese.], and I thought, we need our own monster, and not King Kong, King Kong's adorable. I wanted something that was just insane and intense."[65]

Abrams kept the monster, the film's title, and the plot under wraps until the film's release. The secrets were part of a viral marketing campaign that had people searching the Internet for clues about the film. The campaign started with a nameless film trailer in which an unseen monster decapitates the Statue of Liberty. The only information on the trailer was the film's release date, 1/18/08. The vague film clip led to a wave of questions and speculations by moviegoers and the media. But Abrams refused to say a word.

In the next six months, websites with enigmatic clues appeared—clues designed for individuals like Abrams who enjoy mystery and illusions. One site presented puzzle-piece-like photos of characters from the movie that visitors put together. Another was the website of "Slusho," a fictional drink made from secret deep-sea ingredients, first introduced by Abrams in *Alias*. A third was the website of Tagruato, a fictional deep-sea drilling company that owns Slusho and is connected to the monster. On that website, visitors learned about a deep-sea drilling platform that mysteriously disappeared. Fictional news reports about the drilling platform appeared on YouTube at the same time. Numerous blogs and fan sites also popped up. On these sites, fans shared clues about the movie and the monster. To add to the mystery, Abrams appeared at Comic-Con in July 2007 and passed out Slusho T-shirts but refused to divulge any information about the film.

By the time the film was released, the level of excitement and anticipation among Abrams's fans was very high. As writer Samuel Moon explains:

I was highly invested in this film. I visited all the viral sites, the fan sites, and watched countless YouTube videos building up to the movie's release. . . . I was more excited for *Cloverfield* than just about any movie I had ever seen before or since. After six long months of rumors, speculation and theories, I finally sat down in a pack[ed] theater to watch a shaky cam monster movie that I knew very little about despite the buildup. And I loved it.[66]

Moon was one of many moviegoers who enjoyed the film. Abrams's success on the big and small screen was turning him into a Hollywood legend. It seemed that no matter the challenge, Abrams was up for it. The years to come would test his abilities and lead him in even more directions.

Chapter 5

To Space and Beyond

J. Abrams's ability to successfully take on divergent jobs made him a Hollywood powerhouse. In addition to creating, writing, producing, and directing films and television series, he composed sound tracks, created a video game, and coauthored an innovative novel. And, he took the reins of two of filmdom's most beloved works of science fiction, *Star Wars* and *Star Trek*. No other director had ever directed films from both series, and many fans doubted that one person could successfully handle the job. But Abrams planned to prove them wrong.

In 2006, Abrams was asked to produce and direct a new *Star Trek* movie. The proposed film was the eleventh in the popular series. At first, Abrams was not enthusiastic about the opportunity. He had not been a fan of the television series as a child and was unsure about whether he was the right person for the job: "When I tried to watch the show as a kid, . . . there was a talky, somewhat static vibe that I got from it. I felt it was cold and impersonal and very intellectual. I don't know if I had the brainpower to appreciate it the way my friends did."[67] But since his friends and longtime collaborators Alex Kurtzman, Bob Orci, and Damon Lindelof were writing the script, Abrams reluctantly agreed to produce the film. He refused to make a decision about directing it until the script was complete, although his interest grew with each script meeting.

With his input, the finished screenplay told the kind of mysterious, emotional story that Abrams was known for. When

Abrams directs actor Zoe Saldana on the set of Star Trek *in 2009. The film was nominated for four Academy Awards and won one.*

he showed the completed script to his wife, she loved it and urged him to direct the film. He loved it, too, and signed on to direct. However, because Abrams was not a devoted *Star Trek* fan, his taking the job caused a minor uproar among Trekkies. These die-hard *Star Trek* fans worried that Abrams did not know enough about the series' mythology to make a film that was true to its history. Abrams felt differently: "As someone who wasn't the biggest *Star Trek* fan to begin with, this is probably the last movie I thought I would direct," he explains. "But it was working on the story . . . reading the script, and really feeling the excitement of the story, characters, and action that . . . convinced me that this was something that I didn't need to be a *Star Trek* fan to direct. . . . I discovered when I read the script that I was very excited about it and felt like if I wanted nonfans to go see the movie, that maybe a nonfan should direct the movie."[68]

Granting a Dying Man's Wish

In 2012, the wife of a man named Daniel posted a letter on Reddit.com. In the letter, she explained that Daniel was dying of cancer and had only a short time to live. Daniel was an avid *Star Trek* fan. Before getting sick, he had hoped to see *Star Trek Into Darkness* upon its release in May 2013, but now it was unlikely he would live that long. His dying wish was to see the preview trailer for the film. The trailer was being shown as an accompaniment to the film *The Hobbit* in some theaters. Daniel's wife took him to a theater that was showing *The Hobbit*. Unfortunately, the trailer was not shown in that particular theater.

Unable to fulfill her husband's wish, she turned to the Internet, asking for help. When word of Daniel's situation reached J.J. Abrams, he set up a private screening for Daniel and his wife. The couple thought Abrams was going to show them the preview trailer for *Star Trek Into Darkness*. However, Abrams surprised them by showing them an early cut of the complete movie, fulfilling the dying man's last wish.

Abrams was right. The film, which was released in 2009, pleased both Trekkies and nonfans alike. It was nominated for four Academy Awards and won one. And, it brought many new fans into the fold. In fact, the film was such a success that Abrams went on to produce and direct another Star Trek film, *Star Trek Into Darkness*, in 2013. It, too, was a big hit. In fact, it was the highest grossing film in the series' history.

A Tribute to Childhood

In the next few years, Abrams was involved in the creation of three new television series—*Undercovers, Alcatraz,* and *Person*

Actors Michael Emerson (left) and Jim Caviezel take part in a scene from Person of Interest, *being filmed on a New York City street in 2011.*

of Interest—as well as producing the two films *Morning Glory* and *Mission: Impossible—Ghost Protocol*. Yet, he still found time to write and direct *Super 8*, an original film that he coproduced with his childhood idol Steven Spielberg, creating an experience that Abrams describes as "just the absolute greatest."[69]

Set in 1979, the film follows a group of young people who are making a movie. While filming the movie, they witness a train wreck that releases an alien monster. It was Abrams's most personal work to date, reflecting many of his own childhood experiences. Says Abrams:

> The crazy thing . . . was just how eerie it was to be in the world surrounded by people who looked just like the friends I had at the time I was going to elementary school, wearing the same clothing. Being on the set and seeing magazines, just set dressing, that I would open up and realize, "I read that thing cover to cover." There were constant sense memories, which is very different from doing something like *Star Trek*, which is

all . . . imagination. This was really a revisiting, which was an intent of the movie, but to actually be there day after day in that period was uncanny.[70]

The film also gave Abrams a chance to combine all the elements he loved in a movie—believable characters, emotions, horror, action, and interpersonal relationships. As he explains:

There was a kind of movie that I loved when I was a kid where I would be laughing one minute, crying the next minute, I would be amazed the next, and scared the next. And by the time the movie is over I felt like I had been through this sort of roller coaster of various emotions and it was a wonderful, satisfying thing. The goal of *Super 8* was to try to make a movie that was not just a comedy, not just a horror movie, not just a science fiction film, not just a love story, not just an emotional family trauma or a weird sort of paranoid thriller, but all of them.[71]

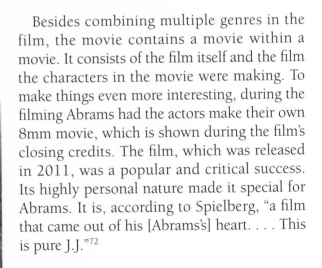

Besides combining multiple genres in the film, the movie contains a movie within a movie. It consists of the film itself and the film the characters in the movie were making. To make things even more interesting, during the filming Abrams had the actors make their own 8mm movie, which is shown during the film's closing credits. The film, which was released in 2011, was a popular and critical success. Its highly personal nature made it special for Abrams. It is, according to Spielberg, "a film that came out of his [Abrams's] heart. . . . This is pure J.J."[72]

Abrams works on the set of his 2011 film Super 8, in which he combines many of the elements he loved in movies as a kid.

A Book Within a Book

Abrams reused the concept of a movie within a movie in the creation of a novel: *S.* is its name. It is essentially a book within a book. Abrams came up with the concept for the novel when he found a paperback book in the Los Angeles airport. The book had a note inside directing the finder to read the book and then leave it in a public place for someone else to find. That gave Abrams an idea for a multilayered, interactive book that is part mystery, part romance, and part puzzles, in which two strangers form a relationship by writing notes to each other in the margins of a book. As he explains,

> The idea came from a very simple place, which is that I was at Los Angeles airport about 15 years ago or so, and I saw a paperback book . . . and I opened it up and someone had written inside, "To whomever finds this book, please read the book, take it somewhere else and leave it for someone else to find it." . . .
>
> It began a thought process for me, which was, what if someone found a book that had extensive notes in it and responded to some of those notes and left the book back?. . . And what if a conversation began strictly in the margins of a novel?[73]

With that in mind, Abrams developed a concept for a book with two plots, the mysterious plot of the inner novel and the story of the relationship that develops between the two readers who attempt to solve the mystery by communicating with each other through handwritten margin notes. Says author Doug Dorst, who collaborated with Abrams on the book, "He wanted to create a book, where you have a novel unfolding in the margins of another novel."[74] To make the book even more unusual, it is stuffed with removable objects, such as old photos, postcards with puzzling messages scrawled across the backs, handwritten letters, notes, a map, and yellowed newspaper clippings, for readers to use to solve the mysteries essential to both plots. Abrams and Dorst worked together for about a year developing the two plots and characters. Then Dorst wrote the book.

The Language of Film-making

The entertainment industry has a language all its own. Here are some common filmmaking terms and their meaning:

antagonist: The villain in a film.

best boy: The name given to the person on a movie set who is responsible for coiling and uncoiling lighting cables.

B-film: A low-budget film.

bit part: A small role for an actor.

cast: All the performers in a film.

crew: Nonactors who work on a movie.

dialogue: Any spoken line in a film.

extra: An individual who appears in a movie in a non-speaking, nonspecific role.

gaffer: The head electrician working on a film.

grip: The person who sets up camera cranes and scaffolding, and moves scenery and props.

hoofer: A dancer.

monologue: A long, uninterrupted speech given by an actor.

outtakes: Camera shots that are not included in the final film.

protagonist: The hero or main character of a film.

shooting: The process of filming a motion picture.

stunt double: A performer who takes the place of an actor during dangerous scenes.

talent: A term that refers to all the actors on a film.

trailer: A short publicity film or film preview.

The book came out in 2013. It was a critical and popular success. It was not easy or cheap to produce. Abrams could have more easily turned the concept into a film or television series. But as a lifelong reader and fan of old-fashioned things, he wanted to present the twin plots in print form. As he explains, "S. was born out of . . . the notion of celebrating the book as an object. . . . The fun of S. is having the book itself. . . . To physically hold it is kind of the point."[75]

A Galaxy Far, Far Away

Working on a novel did not stop Abrams from juggling other projects. In 2013, he was offered the chance to direct *Star Wars: Episode VII*, a reboot of the popular science-fiction series. After doing films in the *Star Trek* and *Mission: Impossible* series, Abrams was looking forward to making an original film. However, as a

boy he had loved *Star Wars*, so he felt conflicted about what to do. As he explains:

The truth is that the *Star Wars* series is something that had such meaning to me as a kid. When they approached me about it, I was insanely flattered but I felt like it was too much. Having done, frankly, you know, *Mission Impossible*

Abrams (top center) leads a read-through of the script for Star Wars Episode VII with the entire main cast. The release of this photo, which includes original Star Wars cast members Harrison Ford, Carrie Fisher, and Mark Hamill, caused a sensation among fans.

and *Star Trek*, I was already involved in a couple of series that pre-existed me, and I wanted to get back to doing original stories.

[But] It was such a once-in-a-lifetime chance to do something truly thrilling and wildly challenging.[76]

Adding to his dilemma was the rivalry that existed between Trekkies and *Star Wars* fans. At the idea of the same person directing films in both series, both fan bases took to social media, where they insisted that it was impossible for one director to do justice to two such different film series. For that reason, and because he still was in the process of finishing up *Star Trek Into Darkness*, Abrams passed on *Star Wars*. But the lure of working on the series he loved did not go away. When his wife urged him to ignore the hubbub and do the film if it was something that he was really interested in, Abrams signed on. Unlike skeptical fans, he felt confident that he could do a good job. In response to their objections, he explained:

It was simply two opportunities to get involved in two disparate film series that are bigger than all of us. I don't feel any kind of Coke vs. Pepsi thing about it. It seems there's enough bandwidth for both of these very different stories to coexist. . . . They feel as different as you could possibly imagine. . . . It's almost like saying these are two movies that take place on Earth, and don't you think they're similar? Because they're about bipeds and vehicles and people living in structures.[77]

His perspective was that he felt "incredibly lucky to be involved in either of them."[78]

Once the filming started, the fan uproar died down, although Abrams had other problems. He assumed that the *Star Wars* film was going to be made in Hollywood, which was not the case. It was going to be made in England, which upset him. The dedicated family man did not want to be separated from his family for an extended period of time. But moving them to England meant he had to take his children out of school, which was not a good solution. To solve the problem, he added sound studios, a special screen used for digital video effects, and other production spaces designed specifically for *Star Wars: Episode VII* to the Bad Robot headquarters. This allowed him to handle much of the film's production in California. The film is scheduled to be released in December 2015.

Helping Others

While filming *Star Wars*, Abrams found a way to use the series' huge fan base to raise money for the United Nations Children's Fund (UNICEF). Abrams offered fans who contributed a

Abrams (left) and actor Brandon Routh attend a 2012 Veterans Day event hosted by The Mission Continues and Got Your 6.

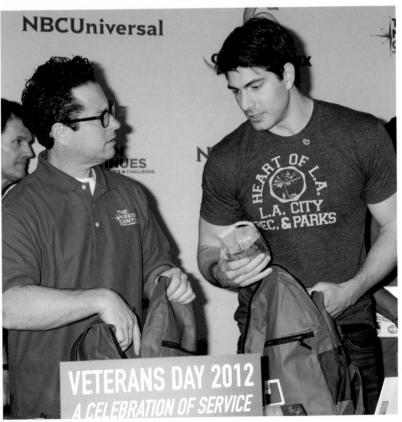

minimum of ten dollars to UNICEF a chance to be entered into a contest in which the grand prize was the opportunity to visit the *Star Wars* set, play a small part in the movie, and participate in an advance screening of the film in the winner's home town. The fundraiser known as Star Wars Force for Change raised $1 million within the first day of its launch.

Force for Change is not the only charity Abrams is involved with. He and his wife support a number of charities, many of which help needy children. For example, in 2013 they hosted a party on the roof of Bad Robot headquarters to raise money for the Children's Defense Fund, a child advocacy group that is dedicated to lifting children out of poverty. As board members of the charity, the couple also read to children in the Los Angeles area public schools. To help children in another way, Abrams created a special mystery box, similar to his childhood possession, that is full of surprises including a set of magic playing cards designed by Abrams. Some of the proceeds from sales of the boxes go to 826 National, a charity that promotes creative writing in public schools.

Abrams and his wife, Katie, are also involved in supporting and helping military families and veterans through the Fisher House and Got Your 6 charities. Fisher House is a network of homes where military families can stay at no cost while a sick or an injured loved one is receiving medical treatment. Got Your 6 connects veterans with leaders in the entertainment industry, helps empower veterans to become community leaders, and raises public awareness of issues concerning veterans. Abrams's involvement in these charities ranges from helping veterans tell their stories on screen to stuffing backpacks for needy families with canned goods and breakfast foods, including the ingredients for Abrams's original cinnamon sugar pancakes, recipe included.

Supporting certain political candidates endorsed by the Democratic Party is another way Abrams and his wife hope to change society for the better. In 2013 alone, the couple donated a total of $117,200 in support of various Democratic candidates. They were also big supporters of Barack Obama's two presidential campaigns and were invited to dine in the White House in 2014 in gratitude for their help.

Into the Future

Between his career, charity work, and family life, J.J. Abrams is a very busy man. On the home front, Abrams and his family moved into a spectacular new home in Pacific Palisades, California, in

Abrams and his family reportedly moved in 2014 into this home overlooking the ocean in Pacific Palisades, California—the town where he grew up.

2014. The 14-million-dollar house sits on 6 acres (2.4ha) and looks out on the Pacific Ocean. It has seven bedrooms and nine bathrooms, a home gym, and a swimming pool.

Abrams and his family spend most of the year in the house. During the summer and long school holidays, they head to Maine, where Katie McGrath grew up. The family recently purchased a 60-acre (24.3ha) lakefront vacation home in Camden, Maine. In addition to relaxing and enjoying waterfront activities while in Maine, Abrams and his wife are involved in supporting local issues aimed at protecting the environment. In addition to vacationing in Maine, Abrams hopes to have some time in the future to travel with his family. He has never been to Israel, India, or Africa and says that he would like to visit these places someday, and that he would like to go back to Japan.

Those trips will probably not happen anytime soon. Professionally, Abrams may be too busy to travel for a while. Although Abrams is renowned for the secrecy surrounding his projects, he has spoken about some of his plans. For instance, he is involved in developing a movie with Gabe Newell, the cofounder of the video game company Valve. It will be based on one of the company's games. Conversely, Abrams has an idea for a video game that he and Newell hope to create together. Abrams is also committed to producing another *Star Trek* film. And, he and Matt Reeves have been discussing making *Cloverfield II*, a sequel to Abrams's horror movie.

In addition, he is working on developing a mystery-adventure movie, a caper movie about a diamond heist, a film about cyclist Lance Armstrong, and a science-fiction movie about radiation exposure. He is also involved in creating a television series based on the 1973 science-fiction film *Westworld*, and a television series about a rock-and-roll band. And these are just a small sampling of his various projects.

Beyond these projects, Abrams is open to most everything. He talks about staging a play, writing a children's book, and making small, low-budget independent films. One thing is certain: he has no intention of retiring or slowing down any time soon. "I feel so lucky that I've gotten to do everything I've done," he admits. "I feel I'm still at an age when a lot of . . . stuff is within reach. Again, it has to be the right thing at the right time. I'm not good at planning five years in advance, but there's still a lot I want to do."[79] For millions of fans all over the world, this is surely good news.

Introduction: The Multi-Hyphenate

1. Quoted in David Segal. "Director J.J. Abrams, Running with the Shows." *Washington Post*, May 5, 2006. www .washingtonpost.com/wp-dyn/content/article/2006/05/04 /AR2006050402074.html.

2. Quoted in Bill Keveney. "The Many Aliases of J.J. Abrams." *USA Today*, January 4, 2005. http://usatoday30 .usatoday.com/life/television/news/2005-01-04-abrams_x .htm.

3. Brendan Reilly. "A Lesson in Branding from J.J. Abrams, Hollywood's Jack of All Trades." March Communications, August 22, 2013, www.marchpr.com/multimedia/2013 /08/a-lesson-in-branding-from-j-j-abrams-hollywoods -jack-of-all-trades.

4. Quoted in IMDb. "J.J. Abrams Biography." www.imdb .com/name/nm0009190/bio?ref_=nm_dyk_qt_sm#quotes.

5. Quoted in Brian D. Johnson. "The Man with *Star Wars* and *Star Trek* in His Hands." *Maclean's*, May 14, 2013. www.macleans.ca/culture/movies/master-of-the-universe.

6. Quoted in Danielle Berrin. "Now It's J.J. Abrams' Turn to 'Trek.'" *Jewish Journal*, May 6, 2009. www.jewishjournal .com/community/article/now_its_jj_abrams_turn_to_ trek_20090506/cover_story/article/israelis_helping_syrian _refugees_in_jordan_balancing_aid_and_diplomacy.

7. Quoted in Jennifer Hillner. "J.J. Abrams, Spymaster." *Wired*, May 2006. http://archive.wired.com/wired/archive /14.05/abrams.html.

Chapter 1: Unlimited Possibilities

8. Quoted in David Kamp. "What You Should Know About: J.J. Abrams: A Panoply of Eccentric Biographical Data re: Filmdom's Premier Pop Auteur." *Vanity Fair*, June 2013. www.vanityfair.com/hollywood/2013/06/jj-abrams-star -trek-14-facts.

9. Quoted in "J.J. Abrams: By the Book." *New York Times*, October 24, 2013. www.nytimes.com/2013/10/27/books /review/j-j-abrams-by-the-book.html?_r=3&.

10. Quoted in Nev Pierce. "Star Child." *Empire*, May 2013, p. 76.

11. Quoted in Pierce. "Star Child," p. 77.

12. Quoted in Pierce. "Star Child," p. 76.

13. Quoted in Stuart Fox. "J.J. Abrams Gets Lost Again." *Popular Science*, August 27, 2008. www.popsci.com/few -questions/article/2008-08/jj-abrams-gets-lost-again.

14. J.J. Abrams. "J.J. Abrams' TED Talk: The Mystery Box." J.J. Abrams Fans, August 18, 2013. http://abramsfans .com/j-j-abrams-ted-talk-the-mystery-box.

15. Quoted in Scott Bowles. "J.J. Abrams Raises Curtain on Scary *Super 8*." *USA Today*, June 8, 2011. http://usatoday 30.usatoday.com/life/movies/news/2011-06-08-jj-abrams -super-8-film_n.htm.

16. Abrams. "J.J. Abrams' TED Talk: The Mystery Box."

17. Quoted in Brainy Quote. "J.J. Abrams Quotes." www .brainyquote.com/quotes/authors/j/j_j_abrams.html.

18. Quoted in Joe Williams. "Abrams Pays Homage to *E.T.*, *Goonies* with *Super 8*." *St. Louis Post-Dispatch*, June 5, 2011. www.stltoday.com/entertainment/movies/abrams -pays-homage-to-e-t-goonies-with-super/article_5b4a9b98 -46ba-5969-99fc-e0100dcd4af1.html.

19. Quoted in Noel Murray. "J.J. Abrams." A.V. Club, September 2, 2008. www.avclub.com/article/jj-abrams -14297.

20. Quoted in Murray. "J.J. Abrams."

21. Quoted in Jessica Furseth. "Interview: J.J. Abrams." *Idol Magazine*, Issue Six. http://idolmag.co.uk/film/interview-jj -abrams.

22. Quoted in Pierce. "Star Child," p. 76.

23. Quoted in Pierce. "Star Child," p. 76.

24. Quoted in "L.A. Confidential." *New York Times*, April 16. 2006. www.nytimes.com/2006/04/16/magazine /16wwln_domains.html?pagewanted=all&module=Search &mabReward=relbias%3As.

25. Quoted in NPR. "J.J. Abrams: The 'Super' Career of a Movie-Crazed Kid." June 13, 2011. www.wbur.org /npr/137108820/j-j-abrams-the-super-career-of-a-movie -crazed-kid?ft=3&f=137108820.

26. Quoted in Katie Puckrik. "JJ Abrams: 'I called Spielberg and he said yes.'" *The Guardian*, August 1, 2011. www .theguardian.com/film/2011/aug/01/jj-abrams-spielberg -super-8.

Chapter 2: Lights, Camera, Action!

27. Abrams. "J.J. Abrams' TED Talk: The Mystery Box."

28. Quoted in Damien Murphy. "Behind the Scenes of *Super 8* with J.J. Abrams." *Scholastic*, November 21, 2011. www.scholastic.com/browse/article.jsp?id=3756726.

29. Quoted in NPR. "J.J. Abrams: The 'Super' Career of a Movie-Crazed Kid."

30. Quoted in Scott Huver. "J.J. Abrams on the Story Behind *Super 8*." NBC Bay Area, May 30, 2012. www .nbcbayarea.com/blogs/popcornbiz/JJ-Abrams-Reels-Out -the-Story-Behind-Super-8-123465989.html.

31. Quoted in Segal. "Director J.J. Abrams, Running with the Shows."

32. Quoted in NPR. "J.J. Abrams: The 'Super' Career of a Movie-Crazed Kid."

33. Quoted in Frank Bruni. "Filmmaker J.J. Abrams Is a Crowd Teaser." *New York Times*, May 26, 2011. www .nytimes.com/2011/05/29/magazine/filmmaker-j-j-abrams -is-a-crowd-teaser.html?pagewanted=all&_r=0.

34. Quoted in Todd Longwell. "The Real Kids of *Super 8*, Part 1." The Longwell Files, July 29, 2011. www.thelong wellfiles.com/blog/category/steven%20spielberg.

35. Quoted in Huver. "J.J. Abrams on the Story behind *Super 8*."

36. Quoted in ICG Staff. "Exposure: J.J. Abrams." *ICG Magazine*, June 9, 2011. www.icgmagazine.com/wordpress /2011/06/09/exposure-j-j-abrams.

37. Quoted in NPR. "J.J. Abrams: The 'Super' Career of a Movie-Crazed Kid."

38. Quoted in NPR. "J.J. Abrams: The 'Super' Career of a Movie-Crazed Kid."
39. Quoted in James Dyer. "My Life in Soundtracks: J.J. Abrams." Empire. www.empireonline.com/interviews /interview.asp?IID=1669.
40. Quoted in James Hoare. "Star Wars Fans Have Night-beast to Thank for JJ Abrams." SciFiNow, January 29, 2013. www.scifinow.co.uk/blog/celebrating-nightbeast-jj -abrams-first-film.
41. Quoted in NPR. "J.J. Abrams: The 'Super' Career of a Movie-Crazed Kid."
42. Quoted in Todd Longwell. "Gerard Ravel and the *Super 8* Festival that Launched J.J. Abrams." *Filmmaker*, November 22, 2011. http://filmmakermagazine.com/34904 -gerard-ravel-and-the-super-8-festival-that-launched-j-j -abrams.

Chapter 3: The Professional

43. Quoted in Todd Longwell. "The Real Kids of *Super 8*, Part 2." The Longwell Files, August 12, 2011. www.the longwellfiles.com/blog/the-real-kids-of-super-8-part-2.
44. Quoted in Bruni. "Filmmaker J.J. Abrams Is a Crowd Teaser."
45. Quoted in Geoff Boucher. "Steven Spielberg: *Super 8* is the First True J.J. Abrams Film." *Los Angeles Times*, June 2, 2011. http://articles.latimes.com/2011/jun/02/news/sns-la -jj-abrams-super-8.
46. Quoted in Chris Serico. "J.J. Abrams Readies for 'Revolution.'" Serico Stories, September 17, 2012. http://serico stories.tumblr.com/post/54286077494/j-j-abrams.
47. Quoted in Serico. "J.J. Abrams Readies for 'Revolution.'"
48. Quoted in the Sarah Lawrence College Facebook page, October 7, 2010. www.facebook.com/sarahlawrence college/posts/162939403733274.
49. Quoted in "Who is J.J. Abrams?" Movieline, December 1, 1992. http://movieline.com/1992/12/01/who-is-j-j -abrams.

50. Quoted in Bruni. "Filmmaker J.J. Abrams Is a Crowd Teaser."
51. Quoted in Serico. "J.J. Abrams Readies for 'Revolution.'"
52. Quoted in Pierce. "Star Child," p. 79.
53. Quoted in Frazier Moore. "A New 'Revolution' from Sci-Fi Mogul J.J. Abrams." The Big Story, October 4, 2012. http://bigstory.ap.org/article/new-revolution-sci-fi-mogul-jj-abrams.
54. Ain't It Cool News. "AICN Exclusive! Moriarty's Review of JJ Abrams Superman Script!!," September 23, 2002. www.aintitcool.com/node/13350.
55. Quoted in NPR. "J.J. Abrams: The 'Super' Career of a Movie-Crazed Kid."

Chapter 4: TV Dynamo

56. Quoted in Joe Marine. "J.J. Abrams: 'It's More Important You Learn What to Make Movies About than How to Make Movies.'" No Film School, May 16, 2013. http://nofilmschool.com/2013/05/jj-abrams-learn-what-to-make-movies-about.
57. Quoted in Pierce. "Star Child," p. 78.
58. Quoted in Berrin. "Now It's J.J. Abrams' Turn to *Trek*."
59. Quoted in Murray. "J.J. Abrams."
60. Quoted in "The Genesis of *Lost*." Lostpedia. http://lostpedia.wikia.com/wiki/The_Genesis_of_Lost.
61. Quoted in "The Genesis of *Lost*."
62. Quoted in Jeff Jensen. "Steven Spielberg and J.J. Abrams Discuss How They Met and Reveal the True Origins of *Super 8*." *Entertainment Weekly*, June 9, 2011. http://insidemovies.ew.com/2011/06/09/super-8-steven-spielberg-jj-abrams.
63. Quoted in Hillner. "J.J. Abrams, Spymaster."
64. Quoted in Stax. "Interview: J.J. Abrams." IGN, May 5, 2006. www.ign.com/articles/2006/05/05/interview-jj-abrams.
65. Quoted in Alex Billington. "Comic-Con Live: Paramount Panel—Star Trek, Indiana Jones IV, and More. . . ."

First Showing.Net, July 26, 2007. www.firstshowing
.net/2007/comic-con-live-paramount-panel-star-trek
-indiana-jones-iv-and-more.

66. Samuel Moon. "1-18-08: A Look Back at Cloverfield
Five Years Later." What Culture, January 3, 2013. http://
whatculture.com/film/1-18-08-a-look-back-at-cloverfield
-five-years-later.php.

Chapter 5: To Space and Beyond

67. Quoted in Johnson, "The Man with *Star Wars* and *Star
Trek* in His Hands."

68. Quoted in "10 Questions with J.J. Abrams." Memory
Alpha, May 12, 2009. http://en.memory-alpha.org/wiki
/Memory_Alpha:Ask_J.J._Abrams/Answers.

69. Quoted in "J.J. Abrams Interview for *Super 8*." Flicks
and Bits, June 9, 2011. www.flicksandbits.com/2011
/06/09/j-j-abrams-interview-for-super-8/12485.

70. Quoted in "J.J. Abrams Interview for *Super 8*."

71. Quoted in Peter Sciretta. "Film Interview: JJ Abrams
Talks *Super 8*, Bad Robot, Lens Flares, *Lost*, Spielberg and
the Mystery Box." Slash Film, June 10, 2011. www
.slashfilm.com/film-interview-jj-abrams-talks-super-8-bad
-robot-lens-flares-lost-spielberg-mystery-box.

72. Quoted in Jeff Boucher. "J.J. Abrams Teams with His
Childhood Hero, Steven Spielberg." Daily Titan, June 6,
2011. www.dailytitan.com/2011/06/j-j-abrams-teams
-with-his-childhood-hero-steven-spielberg.

73. Quoted in NPR Staff. "J.J. Abrams on His Dynasty: Too
Much Power for One Man." NPR, November 17, 2013.
www.npr.org/2013/11/17/245275410/j-j-abrams-on-his
-dynasty-too-much-power-for-one-man.

74. Quoted in Logan Hill. "A Long Time Ago, in a Universe
More Analog." *New York Times*, October 27, 2013. www
.nytimes.com/2013/10/28/books/j-j-abrams-and-doug
-dorst-collaborate-on-a-book-s.html?pagewanted=all&
_r=0.

75. Quoted in Hill. "A Long Time Ago, in a Universe More
Analog."

76. Quoted in NPR Staff, on WBUR. "J.J. Abrams on His Dynasty: Too Much Power for One Man." WBUR, November 17, 2013. www.wbur.org/npr/245275410/j-j-abrams -on-his-dynasty-too-much-power-for-one-man?ft=3&f =245275410.

77. Quoted in Johnson. "The Man with *Star Wars* and *Star Trek* in His Hands."

78. Quoted in Johnson. "The Man with *Star Wars* and *Star Trek* in His Hands."

79. Quoted in Travis. "J.J. Abrams Talks Shop About Filming *Star Wars* and *Star Trek*." popcritica, April 26, 2013. http://popcritica.com/j-j-abrams-talks-shop-about-filming -star-wars-and-star-trek.

1966
Jeffrey Jacob Abrams is born in New York City.

1971
The Abrams family moves to Pacific Palisades, California.

1974
Abrams visits Universal Studios with his grandfather.
Abrams starts making home movies with his parents' camera.

1976
Abrams's grandparents buy him an 8mm camera.

1981
Abrams's film is shown in the Best Teen Super 8mm Films of '81 Festival.
Abrams and Matt Reeves repair Steven Spielberg's home movies.

1982
Abrams composes the score for *Nightbeast*.

1984
Abrams graduates from high school.

1988
Abrams writes *Taking Care of Business* with Jill Mazursky.
Abrams graduates from Sarah Lawrence College.

1991
Regarding Henry is released.

1992
Forever Young is released. Abrams is paid 2 million dollars for the screenplay.

1994

Abrams meets Katie McGrath.

1996

Abrams marries Katie McGrath.

1998

Abrams's son Henry is born.
Abrams starts Bad Robot with Bryan Burk.
Felicity is aired.

1999

Abrams's daughter Gracie is born.

2001

Alias is aired.

2002

Abrams's *Superman: Flyby* script is leaked onto the Internet.

2004

Lost is aired.

2005

Abrams wins an Emmy Award and an American Society of Composers, Authors and Publishers (ASCAP) Award for *Lost*.

2006

Abrams's son August is born.
Abrams directs *Mission: Impossible III*.
Abrams wins an ASCAP Award, a Writers Guild of America Award, and a Producers Guild Award (PGA) for *Lost*.

2008

Fringe is aired.
Cloverfield is released.

2009

Star Trek is released.
Abrams wins an ASCAP Award for *Lost*.

2010

Abrams wins an SFX Award for *Star Trek*.
Undercovers is aired.

2011

Super 8 and *Mission: Impossible—Ghost Protocol* are released.
Person of Interest is aired.
Abrams wins an ASCAP Award for *Person of Interest*.

2012

Abrams's mother dies.
Abrams wins the Saturn Best Director Award for *Super 8*.
Alcatraz and *Revolution* are aired.

2013

Star Trek Into Darkness is released.
Abrams wins the Hollywood Film Award for *Star Trek Into Darkness*.
Abrams wins PGA's Norman Lear Achievement Award in Television.
S. is published.
Abrams wins an ASCAP Award for *Alcatraz*.
Almost Human is aired.

2014

Abrams works on *Star Wars: Episode VII*.
Believe is aired.
Abrams attends a White House dinner.

Books

Peter Barber. *J.J. Abrams 111 Success Facts: Everything You Need to Know About J.J. Abrams*. Brisbane, Australia: Emereo, 2014. This book gives facts about Abrams's career and personal life, and includes links to Internet articles.

Tara Bennett and Paul Terry. *Lost Encyclopedia*. New York: DK, 2010. This book provides all sorts of information about the television series *Lost*, including approximately 1,500 pictures.

Christina Hamlett. *Screenwriting for Teens: The 100 Principles of Screenwriting Every Budding Writer Must Know*. Studio City, CA: Michael Wiese Productions, 2006. This guide to screenwriting provides writing exercises and examples from films, to help teens write original screenplays.

Troy Lanier and Clay Nichols. *Filmmaking for Teens: Pulling Off Your Shorts*. Studio City, CA: Michael Wiese Productions, 2010. A filmmaking guide for teens; it includes information on what happens on movie sets, making short films, budgets, casting, location, and publicity.

Stephanie Spinner. *Who Is Steven Spielberg?* New York: Grossett and Dunlap, 2013. This is a short biography of the director's life.

Torene Svitil and Amy Dunkleburger. *So You Want to Work in Set Design, Costuming, or Make-Up?* Berkeley Heights, NJ: Enslow, 2008. This book gives information about careers as set designers, costume designers, art directors, and hair and makeup artists.

Periodicals

J.J. Abrams. "J.J. Abrams on the Magic of Mystery." *Wired Magazine*, May 2009.

J.J. Abrams. "10 Questions for J.J. Abrams." *Time*, May 18, 2009.

John Anderson. "*Trek* and J.J. Abrams Mind-Meld." *Wall Street Journal*, May 16, 2013.

Jen Chaney. "J.J. Abrams: The Modern Master of Mainstream Sci-Fi." *Washington Post*, June 3, 2011.

Paul Harris. "J.J. Abrams: The Man Who Boldly Goes. . . ." *The Guardian*, April 6, 2013. www.theguardian.com/theobserver /2013/apr/07/profile-jj-abrams-star-wars.

Internet Sources

"J.J. Abrams: On Filmmaking." YouTube. Published on May 8, 2013, by BAFTA Guru. www.youtube.com/watch?v=bN -On2CusDM. YouTube video of an interview with Abrams on May 1, 2013.

"Amplify Mentor Event: J.J. Abrams." YouTube. Uploaded on May 20, 2013, by Jeff Solomon. www.youtube.com /watch?v=Fu5TRZVxweA. YouTube video of an "Amplify" interview on May 20, 2013.

Alex Billington. "Interview: Bad Robot's J.J. Abrams—Writer and Director of *Super 8*." www.firstshowing.net/2011/interview -writer-and-director-of-super-8-jj-abrams . Interview on First-Showing.net, June 20, 2011—just before the *Super 8* movie opened in theaters.

The Famous People. "J.J. Abrams." www.thefamouspeople.com /profiles/j-j-abrams-3353.php. His life history and biography, presented by the Society for Recognition of Famous People.

"The Mystery Box." YouTube. Uploaded on January 14, 2008, by TEDTalks. www.youtube.com/watch?v=vpjVgF5JDq8. YouTube video of Abrams's TED Talk in January 2008.

Smithsonian Collections Blog. "The Summer of *Super 8*." http:// si-siris.blogspot.com/2011/06/summer-of-super-8.html. Blog posting by Karma Foley for the Human Studies Film Archives, about the history of 16mm and 8mm film.

Websites

Bad Robot Productions (www.facebook.com/pages/Bad-Robot -Productions/214632218556454). This unofficial Facebook community page for Bad Robot provides information about the company's films and television series and about J.J. Abrams.

Lostpedia (http://lostpedia.wikia.com/wiki/Main_Page). This is a virtual encyclopedia dealing with everything related to the television series *Lost*.

Memory Alpha (http://en.memory-alpha.org/wiki/Portal:Main). This website is a virtual encyclopedia dealing with everything related to *Star Trek*.

Super8Site (www.super8site.com/museum/index_e.shtml). This website is dedicated to the Super 8 movie camera. It provides all sorts of information about the camera and its history.

Super 8 film experimentation

Best Teen Super 8mm Films of '81 festival, 37–39

family/friends, acting roles, 29–30

film editing, *28*, 37

home movies, 19, 25, *26*

model-building, 28

production multitasking, 27

visual effects, 31

Superman: Flyby (screenplay), 53–54

T

Taking Care of Business (film), 7, 45–48, *46*

TEACH Campaign speech, 44

Trivia, about Abrams, J.J., 62

TV series, created by Abrams, J.J. *See individual TV series*

TV series, favorites of Abrams, J.J., 20, *21*, 22, *22*

The Twilight Zone (TV series), 20, 22, 57

U

Undercovers (TV series), 72

United Nations Children's Fund (UNICEF), 81–82

V

Visual effects, 29, 31–32, 80–81

See also Special effects, interest in

W

War of the Worlds (film), 63–64

What About Brian? (TV series), 7

Barbara Sheen is the author of eighty-six books for young people. She lives in New Mexico with her family. In her spare time she likes to swim, garden, walk, and watch J.J. Abrams's movies and television series.